Life
Interrupted

All proceeds from the sale of this book go to charity
to raise funds for Lymphoma research and clinical trials.

First published in Australia in 2021
by Atlantis Books
48 Ross Street, Glebe NSW 2037
www.littlesteps.com.au
www.atlantisbooks.com.au

Text copyright © 2021 Karina Stell
Cover image © 2021 Jacqueline Stell

A Catalogue-In-Publication entry for this book is available from
the National Library of Australia.

ISBN: 978-1-925839-86-9

Designed by Nina Nielsen
Edited by Katia Ariel
Printed in China
10 9 8 7 6 5 4 3 2 1

KARINA STELL

Life
Interrupted

Atlantis Books

A Note from Karina's Daughters

Our mum began writing this book during her first remission in 2015. Through multiple relapses, treatments, life threatening procedures and eventual palliation, her determination to finish writing never wavered.

Our courageous mum passed away on 27 September, 2018 at home with her children. There will never be words to describe the depth of our love and our loss. All we hope is that her words reach and touch each one of you, wherever you find yourselves on your journey.

We, her children, are forever proud. Forever changed. Forever grateful.

Foreword — by Dr David Joske

It would be glib, but truthful, for me to say I don't know exactly what it's like to be told you have cancer, because I haven't been so diagnosed. However, I do have a fair idea: I have given the bad news many times and talked to patients about their cancer upwards of thirty times a week during my twenty-five years as a haematologist. I know there is, however, a yawning gap between giving versus receiving such news and this is exactly why Karina's book is such a rare and valuable contribution. With her permission, I will tell my side of her story with some asides along the way.

I first met Karina in October 2016 when she came to Perth following the news of a relapse; it was evident she had experienced a complicated course in New South Wales, with an uncommon lymphoma. Initially, Karina had been diagnosed and treated for Hodgkin lymphoma. When relapse was diagnosed from a biopsy of a lymph gland at the angle of the leg, the review by our histopathologists concluded that she now had a peripheral T-cell lymphoma (PTCL). Obviously, this was a source of great distress.

Lymphomas collectively are the fifth most common cancer type affecting Australian adults. T-cell non-Hodgkin lymphomas of various types make up about fifteen per cent of lymphomas overall. They can be technically hard to diagnose even on good biopsy samples obtained at surgery; they have the reputation of being more difficult to treat and cure. PTCL can arise out of Hodgkin lymphoma. Irrespective of its origin though, we tend to treat relapses of Hodgkin and higher-grade non-Hodgkin lymphoma very similarly.

And so, we agreed to embark upon so-called salvage chemotherapy. On a scale of one to ten, rating chemotherapy strength, this treatment is about seven or eight (where a bone marrow transplant is ten). It is hard work, with four days of chemo at a time, and a subsequent dropping of blood cell counts and immune defenses. Some have a harder time than others and for Karina, the nausea was profound and very disabling. I remember how brave she was to commit to the second cycle of treatment after the first had been so tough.

People often say to me that my job must be awful –

giving such horrible treatments, dealing in bad news all the time. I reply that it is a great privilege. I tend to see people at their best, showing great bravery and dignity, and Karina was very much such a person. The lay press portrays people affected by cancer in very emotive terms: 'sufferers' or 'victims' who are 'fighting the battle.' The truth is that cancer is you or I (for Australians who reach seventy-five years of age, one in three men and one in four women), ordinary people, who must come to grips with a shocking and life-threatening illness. For those who are told there is a relapse, there is an awful déjà vu.

My experience is that some assimilate this shock more rapidly than others (indeed, some never do and their currency of communication with me is a language of denial). Often the real mental square-up comes not at the beginning of the journey, but after the hurly-burly of diagnosis, tests and treatment has finished. We are more aware of this now and many practitioners or depart-ments will offer support in the form of a post-treatment debrief, or time with a counsellor.

After the second cycle, Karina's PET scan showed a near-complete response and we proceeded to an autol-ogous bone marrow stem cell transplant. In this procedure, we collect some marrow stem cells from the blood stream (just as the blood counts are recovering from the chemo), and freeze them down. In effect, we now have some bone marrow outside the body. We then give a much bigger dose of chemo, because chemo is mostly limited by the prospect of wiping someone's bone marrow, which would leave them without blood cells or an immune system – they wouldn't last long! Once this bigger chemo dose is metabolised, we infuse the stem cells back like a blood transfusion. Our hope is that they will circulate around the body, recognise the bone marrow as home, set up shop, and start producing blood cells ten or twelve days later.

Karina received the stem cells on 5 January 2017. We were very concerned about the risk of more bad nausea, and how Karina's lungs would cope with this after extensive damage from previous chemotherapy. She did again have a stormy course with various infections and a lot of time in hospital. In fact, she went through hell. Nausea was ongoing and required heavy drug treatments. The kidneys took a hit at one stage, the blood counts were unusually slow to recover, and we picked up a rare viral infection as the cause. Once this was treated, things started to turn around.

At about two months out, she decided to return to NSW and I recommended my colleague Dr Mark Hertzberg, one of Australia's leading lymphoma specialists (we call ourselves 'lymphomaniacs'). The counts still were a bit low and this remained a concern over 2017. We caught up when Karina visited Perth in December 2017. We had a discussion about trying to boost her immune system.

The criticism has rightly been made of the medical profession that we know a lot about wrecking people's immune systems and very little about building them up. I have come to a view on this, which focuses on what I call 'lifestyle management of cancer.' Life experience tells us our immune systems work best when we are happy, productive, sleeping well, eating well, exercising and stress-free. Of course, it's impossible to be perfectly so. But a mental attitude and sensible lifestyle choices can, I believe, help keep the beast under control. (We know now, from several of the new success stories in lymphoma treatment, such as Rituximab for B-cell lymphomas, Nivolumab for relapsed Hodgkin lymphoma, and CAR T-cell therapy, that if we can get the immune cells working well, they can be powerfully directed towards eradicating cancer cells.)

I recall speaking with a patient early during his lymphoma treatment along these lines; subsequently, he decided to reduce his hardware business to just serving retail and not spend his Sundays providing wholesale goods to aggressive and demanding tradies. I believe this slight drop in income but a huge drop in stress levels helped him cope with his treatment and diagnosis. He was grateful for the advice.

Almost 18 months after the bone marrow transplant I learnt from Karina the awful news of a second relapse. I didn't know the medical details but I did know she opted out of further treatment. In fact, she decided to direct her energies to other areas. This might seem a strange decision to some, who assume we must all fight tooth and nail for every second on this planet regardless of cost (not money, but side effects, time in hospital, time away from home, drips, antibiotics, transfusions).

Again, I make a point of saying to people under my care, if things are not going well, they are free to choose when they have had enough. If possible, I have this conversation with family members present, so everyone is aware this has been said out loud. I have regrettably seen people with advanced cancer bash on, their heart no longer really in it, just to please those around them, who of course, don't want them to go. We must all respect the right of a person to choose what path they will take under such extreme duress – provided they have been given clear information upon which to make their choice. I have been referred individuals with lymphoma for a third or even fourth opinion, who have been visibly relieved when I have suggested it might be time to shift the sights from cure to making the best of what time is left.

Another frequent expectation put upon people with cancer is that they must be positive, that they must fight. It surprises people who know me for my role in starting Solaris Cancer Care (an organisation that provides supervised complementary therapies to cancer patients in six centres across Western Australia) that I do not subscribe to this view. There is little evidence that a positive coping style changes cancer outcomes. Moreover, people often feel too exhausted and just too damn rotten to do the brave-face thing, and even feel guilty because of this.

Rather, my advice to those under my care is to get to

a point where you can be *calm* about your situation. When you wake in the morning, and are hit again with the awful realization of cancer and the treatment and the change in life, then you need to be able to say, 'Okay, so I have the medical plan to deal with this, and I understand and agree with it; and then I have my own plan to manage things as well.' (This gets back to the lifestyle management idea I mentioned earlier.) This is very different for different people and it is absolutely a case of horses for courses: meditation, yoga, massage, mindfulness, counselling, research (be wary of many internet chat sites, usually worst-case scenarios) and so on, are not for everyone but if they help, that's great. Our experience with Solaris is that selecting some support of this nature gives people a returning sense of empowerment to be able to self-manage better. If there is any one thing I do recommend, it is exercise, during and after treatment. Not just walking either, but some light resistance work as well. Chemo and steroids dissolve muscle and the only way to keep it, or get it back, is by *using* the muscle. This in turn helps dissipate the strong fatigue that many experience, sometimes even years after treatment has finished.

So, I have tried to impart some of my learnings in telling Karina's story from my point of view. She has told it far better than me. The power and veracity of the lived experience will trump an 'expert' every time. Whether you read this book as a patient, as a carer or as an interested health professional, I am sure you will come away with a deeper and more heartfelt appreciation of the fleeting, precious beauty of life. Shakespeare's poor player, strutting and fretting his hour upon the stage indeed. I commend Karina for her candour, her courage and her care for others – she chose to share her difficult hour on stage with us all.

David Joske

Clinical Haematologist, Sir Charles Gairdner Hospital Clinical Professor of Medicine, UWA.

1 August 2018

Preface by Karina Stell

I've decided to write this book, as painful as it is for me, because I know there are others, like me, who have faced the unimaginable, and wondered how to begin living their lives again. Whether you are the sufferer, or the loved ones of those who suffer with cancer, it can feel the same: helplessness and vulnerability, a dramatic shift from a life once known.

Cancer has been my companion for most of eight years, and to be honest, I'm not sure whether this is where it ends or whether we have further to travel together. I'm in remission. A year now. Holding on to life feels very slippery. It never stops being frightening for me and I wanted to share this book, as I say, because I know there are others just like me. The minute they have a diagnosis, cancer patients are set apart from their world. How does one live when there is nothing certain, when it becomes very real that tomorrow is not guaranteed, but you so much want to be a part of the carefree living that once existed?

I've learned a lot in these eight years, most of all to trust my instincts. They led me to Prof David Joske, whose whole-person approach to cancer treatment took me from absolute despair (on my third diagnosis) to finding that human connection between medical team and patient I had been looking for. Each person has particular needs that must be met in order for them to feel safe. Until I found it with Prof Joske, treatment was more than I could bear. The emotional tangled up with the physical and it was important to me that both were acknowledged as part of the disease. I owe him more than words can demonstrate and I feel driven to share this fundamental learning: finding the right team can ensure the heart is held while the body is ravaged.

I am sure that the emotions I felt with each of my three diagnoses have been experienced by every other soul who has been delivered this horrifying news. First a gynecological cancer followed by two blood cancers for me, each diagnosis increasing the shadow I lived under. My hope is if others become connected to the experiences that I went through, the things that I learned along the way, it may create a feeling of 'me too!' which makes living with this disease less lonely. Being understood is the emotional *everything*. Platitudes are painful, and if one person learns to never say 'stay positive' or 'you can't give up' to someone with cancer, writing this book will have been worth it.

I hope the reading of my story creates a soft place for those who are suffering with this disease, and also for those who have loved ones that are suffering; for all involved to just feel understood. Many books have been filled with positive affirmations and stories of survival against the odds. I found these hard to relate to. Instead, I wanted others to understand how it felt to live with cancer, wondering whether I was going to win or lose this battle and still be a mother, daughter, sister and friend. This book is for those who are also wondering. A fellow traveller's story of living with uncertainty and learning to trust herself.

With love, Karina

What I Thought I Knew

I've always been an organiser. In fact, my former employer of over twenty-five years had said, every business needs a Karina. That makes me smile. Organisation was, and still is, a pet joy. It has helped me feel in control of the world and more specifically my life. Give me anything that needs sorting and I come alive. As a little girl, I would collect my father's opened envelopes and put them in one of my mother's old handbags, and walk my fingers over the top of them, pretending I was filing. It was intrinsic in me and it made me feel happy and safe. Order in the world. No surprises.

However, in my fifties, life took a left turn; after thirty years as someone's wife, I became divorced. Never in my wildest dreams could I imagine I would be divorced, even though I knew I wasn't happy. It just seemed that marriage was something we are meant to succeed at no matter what. But like most couples facing unhappiness, we tried until it became obvious that there was no point trying any longer – some things were just beyond our control. Surprisingly, the relief of letting go and accepting the previously denied reality was enormous. I learned from this relief – no matter how hard one might deny things, it makes not one bit of difference. They remain like an unwelcome visitor until accepted and dealt with. As much as I now know this to be an absolute, on my cancer journey I have sometimes closed my ears to what felt innately uncomfortable and went along in order to keep others happy. Let's be honest, what did I know about cancer treatment that I should say no to a doctor's opinion? It's hard to separate the fear from the emotional discomfort letting you know something isn't right for you. This was something that took me a long time to understand but giving my instincts the respect they deserved began to govern how I managed each unexpected twist and turn.

The time of my divorce put me on the path of acceptance of the uncontrollable, of listening to my heart. However, the lack of control I felt with cancer was beyond anything I had previously experienced and this hit me hard. Trying to accept what this illness would require of me filled me with terror. I looked for a way around, under and away from it. When all these attempts proved futile, I had to surrender to the fact that this was to be my journey and I had to walk it, like it or not.

Each time I had a new diagnosis my belief in tomorrow would diminish just a little more. It is said, by those who I respect most in the world of this disease, that hope is imperative. Perhaps, but how does one find it when none is felt? For this reason, I believe platitudes harm so deeply. I would rather hear someone tell me that they find themselves without words than to make feel-good statements that fail to grasp the emotional dislocation felt by someone suffering with cancer. Platitudes do nothing to create hope; they leave one feeling alone. Particularly on the days that follow the news of a diagnosis. These days are grief-filled and probably every one of the stages of grief – denial, bargaining, anger, depression and hopefully, in time, acceptance – bounce around within the spirit of the recipient of this news. I now know that grief will take as long as it takes. There's no rushing what the heart needs in order to arrive at the door of acceptance. At least enough acceptance to place one foot in front of the other to walk the formidable path of treatment.

There are many things I wish I had known from the beginning: what I could say yes to, what I should say no to, and that this illness, for some time at least, has belonged to me. I have learned that acceptance does not mean blind agreement. I have needed to advocate for myself and not just accept invasions into my body without understanding why they are being performed. And whilst physically controlling this disease is not always in our hands, the internal, emotional path we take is up to us. When a dear friend shared with me the following quote from Viktor Frankl, a Holocaust survivor, it touched my heart so deeply. I let these words sink deeply into my soul and have called on them, when needing courage, many times since.

'Everything can be taken from a man but one thing: the last of the human freedoms – to choose one's attitude in any given set of circumstances, to choose one's own way.'

These words do not mean I have to be some sort of hero or inspire others in this battle. What they have meant to me from the day I embraced them, and very specifically when I have undergone treatment, is that if I can't be authentic, if I can't share what is actually going on for me, I am not going to survive emotionally. Physical survival is one thing. I shake before the mystery of what is written for me. But my emotional survival is just as important, and the only way this can even be a possibility is for me to be real. There are no prizes for being heroic in any part of this journey. Our salvation is to be real, and for others to hold us in that really scary place and try and understand what it might be like.

We grasp at the statistics given by our doctors with both hands, always wanting to believe that we will be the percentile that is victorious, whilst underneath asking ourselves why we should be so special. These are the hopes we place in our doctors and our medical team. Every word they utter is collected and repeated to every family member to instill hope and belief that this is a disease that can be beaten.

The doctor–patient relationship is hugely important. For this reason, I wish to say out loud that sadly, some doctors can appear remote from their patients' emotional experience. Some seem beguiled by their own academic pursuits and forget there is a human being connected to the disease that fascinates them so. The same can be said for some nursing staff. After eight years, I can say I know as much, if not more, about how to manage the side effects of treatment of my disease as some nurses. I have learned that a drug won't work very well if given to me a certain way. I know which drugs do not work at all. Cancer patients become experts in their disease. Some nurses forget this and feel incensed when patients offer this sort of knowledge. These are not many, but in eight years I have met a few; it's painful and can take the sense of autonomy and self-respect from a patient fighting for their life.

I believe that the very best doctors and the very best nurses walk alongside their patients throughout treatment, not ahead of them. They talk with them, not at them or down to them. Humanity. Compassion. Connection. Respect. These qualities help cancer sufferers countenance the nameless ghost they see in the mirror, particularly when treatment has thoroughly distorted their physical being.

I have been privileged to have some amazing people as part of my care team and I remember every single one of them with warmth and gratitude. But for those few who are excited by academia more than humanity, or who can't connect with the withered body resulting from disease and treatment, or who listen but don't really hear, please take pause, and be grateful that there but for the grace of God, go you. Cancer does not play at what it does. It has an agenda that when implemented, kills its host. If you can imagine what it feels like, day in and day out, when in the early hours of the morning nausea hits or when blood results are threatening, and the body starts to fail, you will offer your patients something more valuable than any academic achievement. You will offer them empathy; human connection.

When I hear of any cancer story now, I don't think of anatomy. I think about what it must have been like the day their life changed. The fear, the denial, the lack of hope that would come and go. I always want to internally say hello to them. To say via my own wounded heart to theirs, *I know.*

The Shot from Nowhere

It had been an ordinary day in late 2009 when life was interrupted. I had only been separated for a matter of months. Life was good. I had moved from my marital home into a new unit with my youngest daughter and was studying to become a therapist. I was loving studying again and the feeling of achieving. I was learning to enjoy life outside the stresses of an unhappy marriage and I started to reflect on what I wanted my life to be about and what really mattered to me. These months grew a feeling of meaning and fulfillment.

However, on a September evening, a seemingly simple discovery put an end to all of this and life took a far more urgent turn. I kissed my daughter goodnight and left to go to bed. Just before I popped into bed, I went to the bathroom. I noticed a stinging when I emptied my bladder. It hurt enough that I remember screwing up my face at the discomfort. It was impossible to see anything, so I had a shower hoping the soothing warm water would help the stinging subside. As I washed myself, I felt a lump between my legs. About the size of a jelly bean, and it was painful to touch. I tried to downplay its significance. One never thinks cancer could be a reality although most seem to fear it constantly. It's a funny contradiction. I wanted reassurance even though I couldn't imagine something so small could cause too much mischief. I vacillated between thinking things would be fine and the feeling that this was the beginning of something very frightening. I slept fitfully that night. The sooner I could see my doctor, the better.

I had a new GP since my separation. She was kind, warm and very thorough. I explained my experience the evening before and she gestured for me to hop up onto the examination table. I lay there as she examined me, praying for the usual 'Oh, its nothing,' that we most often hear. There was a lengthy silence. In fact, those words of reassurance never came. What I began to sense was that all was not well. Suddenly, the silence was broken and there was a flood of conversation, from her to me and from her to other doctors over the phone, about who I should go and see and how quickly I could get in. I heard the mention of cancer but it all seemed garbled and nonsensical to me. My doctor's serious face was terrifying. Her voice started to fade into the background as my thumping heart seemed to take over my ears. I started to shake. Hearing cancer and my name in the same sentence as she spoke to someone on the phone was startling. Like all newcomers to this experience, I could only imagine death. That's all that went around and around in my head. I could hear that I was to see someone. I knew so little about what would come next. Just the words 'Oh, please no,' seemed to repeat inside me.

Over the course of the consultation, I managed to focus more. I seemingly was booked in to see a surgeon the following day. Beset by sadness and anxiety, I left the GP's surgery utterly confused as to how this could be happening. The anticipation of telling my girls was painful. Separations are hard on everyone in a family, I thought, and to now give them news like this seemed so unfair. It would prove to be a difficult conversation.

*

The professor who was to operate on me was an elderly

and empathic man. The best worldwide, they told me. He had dedicated his life to studying a disease I didn't even know existed. He was to remove what was eventually identified as a squamous cell carcinoma. Vulvar cancer. This was the commencement of an education I never wanted. He told me removal should be straightforward. A perimeter needed to be taken to get it all. But had it reached the lymph nodes? No way of knowing until surgery. Lymph nodes. The way in which cancer travels around the body and spreads, I had once read. Dear God, please don't let this be. My heart hurt so deeply, and I felt such sorrow at what I may lose. The people I loved, and my life cut short at fifty-one. How on earth have I found myself here, I thought.

Within days I had a resection of the affected area. I woke after surgery catheterised and in some discomfort, but my morphine pump spared me physical and emotional pain. Nothing was known yet and I had to wait for pathology to learn whether my lymph nodes were clear or not. The days this took seemed like weeks. I was thankful that my morphine pump gifted me with sleep and along with visiting family and close friends, the time eventually passed.

Some days later, I heard my surgeon greeting the nurses on the ward and his footsteps as he moved toward my room. He stopped in the doorway, wished me a good morning and walked over to my bedside. I chatted briefly about how I felt and how comfortable I was, all the time wanting to hear just one thing. He must have seen it in my eyes as he took my hand and patted it and said, 'It missed your nodes by a few millimeters. I don't think we'll take them. I think this should be the end of it and I'll see you in a few weeks.' My face became warm and I suddenly became so tired. Tears filled my eyes and I felt myself start to sob. My eldest, Kate, 29, my middle girl, Elisabeth, 26, and my youngest, Philippa, 24, were in the room and we all cried with relief. I saw the weight leave their eyes. These women in their early adulthoods had watched their parents in deep unhappiness for many years, endured our separation and now had felt the terror that comes with a cancer diagnosis. I prayed I could spare them any more days like these.

*

It was uncomfortable after surgery for quite some time,

but this paled into nothing when compared with my greater fear of lymph involvement. I went home and tried to resume life as best I could while I healed. If this was to be my brush with cancer, I would have said at that time that I had got off easily. I was watched post-op very carefully both by my surgeon and my gynecologist. I prayed this would keep me safe.

However, each three months brought concern, both to my doctors and, in turn, to me. Each checkup, I would have a colposcopy and a biopsy and every one of these would show advanced pre-cancer cells developing. (What I did not know at the time was this would be the case every single time for four years.) It became apparent that cancer, even the size of a jelly bean, could be very tenacious. And so there were more resections, a cone biopsy and removal of my cervix. Still the cells persisted. Each visit held the hope that this time maybe the test would be clear, but it never was.

My gynaecologist was amazing. She was full of compassion and understanding that this unrelenting outcome was exhausting. So often I was told that I had a poor immune system that just couldn't fight on my behalf against the virus that created these cells. Many times, to any medical person who would listen, I would ask the question about how an immune system can be strengthened. The answer was always, sadly, that not much could be done.

Despite this being a time where medicine was advancing at an amazing pace, a time of valuable and fascinating research, it was clear that there were some fundamentals that doctors either don't know or couldn't fix. And so, in helping a person improve their immune system, a system that when faulty allows broken cells to proliferate, nothing much could be done. My hands had begun to be covered with flat warts that no amount of treatment could kill. A poor immune system, I was told again. This was a terrifying recurring piece of news. I was frustrated by my body's failure to protect me.

I felt I had no guard at the gate. It felt personal, with nothing protecting me from a disease that was seemingly trying to overrun me. I felt guilt reacting to my body this way. At the same time, I felt angry it had left me exposed. I'm sure I'm not the first to feel this way and it was the beginning of the mixed bag of guilt, gratitude, disappointment and hope that would spin endlessly around for years to come.

By 2013, less than four years after my initial diagnosis, my doctors decided they would carry out a hysterectomy in the hope that they could remove the possibility of any disease invading my uterus. It was a hopeless time. How much of my body would be cut away to try and outrun this seemingly committed attack of cancer cells? I was just about to move house and my doctor agreed to wait until after the move. I needed a break. I was starting to develop a dreadful nausea after anaesthetic with each new operation, so each intervention was not just the surgery, but the recovery days filled with a feeling of motion sickness. Moving was a welcome distraction and it felt like a breath of new life to leave the medical world for a while.

*

I had always wanted to live in a unit in a busy hub, amongst the throb of people and life. Where I could be alone when I wanted, but also walking distance from department stores and the hustle and bustle of people. Philippa had recently left to live in London with her boyfriend for a while. So, this was to be me, on my own, for the first time in my life.

I had looked forward to this move for several years as I had bought off the plan, and when the time arrived, I was excited. I had been suffering from a lingering chest infection for some months and it was unusual that I couldn't shake it off. This was a body hint that something untoward was happening. The day of the move was exhausting. However, I was in my organisational element, unpacking and creating my new home, even though I had noticed not feeling myself. I was gaining weight very easily and there was swelling in my limbs. I hadn't understood what my body was telling me, but as I look back now, I recognise it was the beginning of its failure to cope with the new illness that was about to rear its head. Although had I known, what could I have done?

The unpacking took me over a week and I forgave myself as I was now fifty-five and assumed my age and my increasing weight was slowing me down. Once the move was complete, I didn't have much time to enjoy the life my new location brought. My doctor asked me to prepare for surgery. I had great hopes that I would start to feel my old self again in time. I thought that perhaps my uterus was diseased and that's why I felt so different.

I hoped the surgery would hold some answers.

The removal of my uterus was not painful and my time in hospital seemed to come and go quickly. But recovery was not so easy. It seemed to take me a long time and I felt constantly tired and pale. However, I felt hopeful that this would put an end to cancer cells and the anxiety over each result that showed them once again. However, the vitality I had hoped for did not return. Again, it seemed my body was struggling to cope.

My uterus had shown no disease and in spite of that being a good thing, it didn't explain the origin of persistent positive biopsies. How long was this cycle to repeat itself? There were only my ovaries remaining. It was disheartening. Still, I noticed myself learning to live with this uncertainty. Each check discovered further development of pre-cancer cells, I had no control and my poor doctor felt at a loss. However, I begun to accept that this was, for now, how it was going to be. It started to fall within my 'normal'; my capacity to accommodate uncertainty was expanding.

Just as I surrendered to this new way of living, and almost four years to the month from my first diagnosis, I had begun to notice a niggling pain in my lower back.

Maybe I had wrenched it? I gave it some time, but it seemed to get more painful, not less. It just seemed one thing too many. My frustration with my tiredness, and now the sore back, made me think it was time I had a holiday. I wanted to give my body a real chance to recover, to be somewhere where I could just rest and swim. I booked five days in Fiji and although the thought of travelling internationally on my own for the first time was a little confronting, I knew I had to embrace being single, to start doing these things on my own.

As the holiday approached, there had been little improvement in my energy, and the niggling pain in my back had become uncomfortable enough that it was now waking me at night. Fiji was only two days away, so I decided to have myself checked out. An appointment with my GP the next day raised the possibility that perhaps I might have a kidney stone or cracked rib. Best to have a CT scan to make sure. Could I go today? Tempted to say no, I relented and said I'd go. The thought of passing a kidney stone whilst on holiday in Fiji felt unappealing to say the least. Kate came with me to have the scan and we innocently chatted as we sat in the waiting room, never imagining it could be anything too serious. I had become hypervigilant in monitoring any changes surrounding the vulvar cancer and we felt somewhat safe in knowing we had a close eye on it. It never crossed our minds that something far more insidious could be silently growing at the same time. Eventually I was called in and had a scan of my chest. Even though I had the scan in the morning, it took most of the day to get my results. At 4pm that afternoon I had the results and the scan in my hand. Both Elisabeth and Kate were with me by then.

My GP had asked me to ring her and let her know what the report said, as I wouldn't be able to see her until I came back from holidays. I opened the envelope and started reading. The words felt like a slap and my shock caught in the back of my throat as I tried to read aloud. 'Oh please, not again,' was what my shaking limbs were saying. I remember something about query masses in the background in the chest and a mass around the spinal column. A repeat full body CT was suggested to confirm a *query. Query lymphoma*.

The arrival of more cancer news, query or not, stopped my heart. I could feel my brain scrambling to make sense of what I had just read, at the same time trying to read anything that exempted me or at the very least, gave me hope, that this could be a mistake. I entered into a panic-driven craziness, searching frantically for a way out. I had heard of lymphoma. In my ignorance, I remember thinking there was a good one and a bad one. I didn't know why I thought that, or what that meant, but this ill-informed fragment that I plucked from somewhere in my memory was all I had to cling to.

My eyes darting around the report, the voices of my children in the background in disbelief, time seemed to stand still. We walked the short distance home in a drunk-like meandering. As we arrived, each of us moved to their own spot on the couches. I realised we all felt equally detached from each other. As we sat in the living room, we said very little for a very long while. Finally, I spoke. 'This is bullshit,' I said angrily. 'What are we doing? 'Query' lymphoma, it had said, not 'definite' lymphoma. Why am I being so ridiculous and losing my head?' As I shared my indignation, I saw some hope in my daughters' eyes. I saw how much my responses affected them. My maternal instinct pulled itself away from the child-like fear I was experiencing, and I remembered that this was not just about me. Their terrified eyes reminded me

I was their mother, that I was to be the holder (not only the one being held) through this experience. We found our courage that night, in what I think we all knew was a lie. But for now, the truth was just too much to bear. By nightfall we had convinced ourselves that it was a mistake that would be proven so. We left each other promising to 'think positive.' Words that now make me feel so much indignation when spoken to me. But we were new to this game. It gave us time to process. In our heart of hearts however, I believe we all knew: cancer had outrun me again.

Thinking Positive

The next day I sat on an airplane in a numbed state, telling myself that I needed this holiday, that all that happened the day before was a result of a rushed examination and when I got home I would investigate this properly and it would be proven to be something simpler and kinder. I'd been so tired. I couldn't let a probable error in a radiological report consume me. I had to believe all would be well and that this would in time seem funny. And we would laugh at how quickly we jumped to the worst conclusion. This is how gentle endings are supposed to go. A terrible mistake, cries of relief and off we go promising to think of those not so lucky after we have been chastened by such a close call. Maybe a vow to give to cancer research to assuage our guilt about being healthy.

I arrived in Fiji at night. My hotel was just beautiful, flamed lanterns illuminating the pathway that led to the external reception area. The weather was warm, and I could hear the sea crashing in the distance. I was so happy to be in this paradise. I had made the right decision in coming. The more deeply the surroundings pervaded my senses, the more strongly I believed the scan had been a horrible mistake; I was grateful to be alive. Apart from some tiredness and a probable pinched nerve in my back, I was going to be okay.

The mind is a powerful thing. You can believe anything if you want to badly enough. I let my girls know I had arrived safely and my elevated mood helped them feel relief. It also implicated them in the fairytale we all wanted to believe so much.

The relaxation and rest were welcome, and timely. Although I did not know this yet, my body was to face a chemical onslaught in the near future and rest was the best prescription for now. I spent most of my time by the pool reading, watching children play with each other and their parents. The sounds of children playing in a pool are to me the most beautiful sounds and I have always loved hearing them when on holiday. Once again, this sound of carefree happiness reminded me of when my three were little and screaming with excitement, enjoying the water.

The staff were so friendly and kind and it was hard

not to be relaxed and happy, even though there was a heaviness on my chest that I consciously decided to ignore for now. As I was walking back to my room one afternoon, one of the tall handsome Fijian porters walked alongside me for a while. I said 'bula', as was the Fijian custom to greet almost everyone. He responded in kind. He asked me had I been enjoying myself. I said, 'Yes, it is beautiful.' Was I travelling alone? Yes, I was. Did I have a husband? Now, at times, I can be the most naïve of creatures. Putting someone in a uniform somehow leads me to believe them to be beyond the usual human foibles. I believed they would always act properly, and I found myself being quite open in my answers whereas had he been in regular clothes, I would have been quite nervous about this degree of curiosity. I was divorced, I answered. What followed still makes me laugh to this day. 'Have you ever tried a Fijian?' he asked. 'A Fijian what?' I said. He stood still, as did I, so I could catch what he would answer. 'Just a Fijian,' he said.

Wow, I thought. I had been living a parallel life for so long that I couldn't even recognise a proposition when I got one. I was so nervous and unfamiliar with male attention unless from a male in a white coat with a worried look on his face. I quickly and idiotically said, 'Oh, I'm good, thanks!' and scurried back to my room where I just laughed and laughed whilst intermittently hiding my head under my pillow with embarrassment. How alive one feels when really belly laughing. It was so wonderful and cathartic. I spent the rest of the holiday skirting around him. When I saw him, I would think what an idiot he must consider me, all the time giggling to myself like an embarrassed schoolgirl. I owe that man a great debt. He reminded me, at a time when it was very important, that I wasn't dead yet.

As the days passed by, I witnessed three weddings. Beautiful young people starting out in life with all the expectation of joy, striving together, raising a family and being healthy enough to enjoy each other's company. I sat and thought how wonderful that was. I wouldn't want anything less for my children. Untarnished hope. What a wonderful thing. The irony was that I only recognised this incredible gift once I no longer had it. I spoke daily to my girls and they laughed so hard at my behaviour around my Fijian friend. I'm so glad they could laugh too. It was so good for them, just like it had been me.

On the flight home I started to lose faith in my happy

ending. *My* hope had been tarnished, unlike that of the wonderful young people I had witnessed in the days before, and I started to think deeply about what I may have to face. What my girls may have to face. I felt melancholy more than anything else. The holiday had done a lot to mellow me. I was no longer frantic but just very, very sad. I felt courage in those hours on the plane, to do what I may have to do, and at the same time a lot of fear. I resolved to return home and sit my girls down and tell them if this turned out to be bad news, we had to be honest about how we feel, unlike our last time together. If it got too much for anyone and they needed to pull back, then that is what they should do. If my hair was to fall out and they wanted to laugh, they could. I want everyone to be real, because then I could be real. There was no other way to make it through.

I arrived back in Sydney and made my way home, trying to sit with the many emotions going through my body. I knew the next morning I was to have my CT and there would be fewer mysteries, even if I did not find all the answers I needed. Maybe for the scan to show nothing was too much to ask for, but a benign result, yes, a benign result, that was doable.

A Time for Answers

I sat in the waiting room of the same radiology practice the day after my return, but this time, I felt solemn. I can't remember now whether I went alone, or someone was with me. All that stands out is that the girls were with me when the results finally were typed. I had gone back three times that day and each time was turned away as my results weren't ready. It was grueling waiting for what I hoped was a moment of relief. I just wasn't equipped for another troubling outcome – that couldn't be my story, surely.

Later that afternoon, the results were in my hand. I know I should have waited to take them to my GP, but there was no more patience within me. I had to know. With Kate and Elisabeth anxious by my side, I gingerly opened the envelope, scared that evidence of opening it first would cause me to be in some sort of trouble. Crazy, when I think of it now. This envelope held the answers about my life. Of course I would open it! I looked down the scan envelope sleeve, hoping for a short report. I had worked for a radiologist in my twenties and knew a short report was a good report. My heart thumped. It was long. I knew this didn't bode well for me. I pulled it out and read what in short said, there was little doubt I had lymphoma. Several tumours in my chest cavity, one around my airway, one around my spine and one in my left hip.

The girls and I were sitting on a bench in the heart of my home suburb. Overcome with grief and confronted with what we had worked so hard to deny, we just sobbed. To passers-by it must have been unnerving. However, being amongst the crowds did little to contain us. I know for me the pain was searing. I had no faith I could cope with what was to come. Once again, the deafening shock came. Sounds and people disappeared and urgency was all I felt. Where could I run? Where could I go? Like before, I came back to the moment and saw the pain in my children's faces. I wanted to reassure them and yet I found myself falling apart in front of them. I rang my brother Rick, a doctor across the country. As I sat with my girls, I said to him with my voice shaking, 'I think I'm going to die.' Rick's words, minor in their content but huge in their emotion, were, 'No, no, not today, darling.' He asked me to read the report to him. He asked me to find some courage. Could I manage to try and stay calm until I had seen my doctor? I would try, I said. The three of us, stunned and terrified, walked back to my home and held each other and cried again and again. Philippa was due home any day. I had hoped to have a party to welcome her back. Instead I was to share news I would have given anything not to deliver.

I called my GP. She let me know she would arrange for me to see a haematologist the following Tuesday and that I should try and not worry until then. Big ask. The girls and I talked quietly about what this would mean for us all. We cried, and talked, and cried. Tears never seemed to run out. Kate was about to move interstate and told me she would stay. I said no. This disease was going to take enough from us. But we weren't going to let it take everything. I told my girl to go with my blessing. It was important to me. She could fly back whenever she wanted but it mattered to me that her world didn't stop because I was sick. We then heard from Philippa that she was to arrive home the next day. I felt so sad she was coming home to such grief. Like any child who is loved, she no doubt expected to come back into the arms of her family with excitement and joy and curiosity as to what her trip had held for her. Instead she would come home to sadness and fear. The significance of her return had changed from being all about her to being all about me. What guilt that held!

That night Elisabeth stayed with me. We talked in bed about how unreal this felt. How afraid we both were that I might die. We talked about taking one step at a time, so we could manage the news incrementally rather than in one big gulp. We resolved to be there for each other so we could get to wherever the other side of this horror was.

During the night one of us would wake up and cry. The other would hear and we would hug and promise each other it was going to be okay. This was repeated many times over, until it was morning. As we woke and looked at each other, words were not necessary. We knew we had to face another difficult day, but we would do it together.

The next day was the day I had to tell my eighty-six-year-old mother and my youngest daughter that there was every probability that I had a new type of cancer. Not overt like last time, but a more secretive and perhaps a more sinister one that grows and multiplies quietly inside. My father had passed away from stomach cancer eight years earlier. My mother still missed him terribly. How was I supposed to tell her now that her daughter had cancer? The steps into her home were labored and I was so upset to bring her news that no parent should hear. As expected, it hurt her a lot. Elisabeth and I sat with Mum until she felt she understood where we were at with everything and we both hugged her and left.

Later that afternoon my brother Dean rang me distraught. Mum had let him know. My older twin brothers and I, at this time, were all in our fifties. Not babies. But the helplessness we all felt was childlike. I comforted him, he comforted me. We were lost and only knew we wanted to be together as I faced this. Rick also rang me and tried to give me some idea of what lymphoma was, how it was treated and what I could expect. It was intimidating, however, I felt blessed to have so much love around me. How lonely these days must be for some who have no one. I thanked God for giving me a loving family to help me through.

That evening Philippa flew home. With nowhere else to stay until they found a flat, her boyfriend returned to his parents' home and Kate brought Philippa to mine. Joy at seeing my baby girl again, mixed with guilt at breaking her heart, filled that evening. I was beset by the unnerving news my daughter had to digest, just like her older sisters before her, and my guilt for being the source of her grief. It was new to me that evening, but in time it would become more and more familiar. Humbling guilt at not being able to make their world worry-free, at least as much as it related to me. Youth is meant to be a time of having fun, friends and excitement at increasing freedoms. My daughters would have worry as their travelling partner, their mother's sickness invading their youth. I felt such pain watching, yet I was as powerless as they to change anything.

These were the tentacles of cancer, I realised. It was not just physical suffering. I was their mother. I'd spent my life trying to soften their path and be their safe place when life got too much. But that night brought the beginning of what was to become a constant. A hospital admission on someone's birthday, weakness interfering with the fuss of Christmas, devastating news distracting from a homecoming. Early on everyone seems too stunned by the diagnosis to notice, but in time, days, weeks and years become full of spoilt moments. These losses would show in my children's faces no matter how hard they tried to disguise them. Nothing was to be done on this night of Philippa's return, or any other such occasion in the years ahead. There was only the hope that the day would come when I could be their strong, safe place once again.

In the days that followed while we waited for that Tuesday appointment, insanely, we seemed to find things to laugh about. Maybe we felt we could, just for a few days, let go. Try and have fun. Try and be normal. Perhaps a human being cannot stay in such sadness beyond a certain amount of time. We cried with laughter at times and it felt so good to let the tension ease, like a pressure cooker valve that had been opened.

Being human is such a mystery. I would not have expected to have these days of fun, but I am thankful for them, however they happened.

*

Finally, Tuesday morning came and we all tried to appear strong. We sat in a waiting room which was full of people in various stages of illness. Some looked quite ill and thin, with dark circles around their eyes, some smiling and chatty with friends, their heads and faces completely hairless. Like everything else, the tangible evidence of this disease scared me.

I was eventually called in. My doctor appeared an unassuming man with a pretty, young woman at his side. His registrar, I later found out. He was supposed to be very good. I could only trust because what did I know? We discussed that it appeared I had lymphoma, but it would be necessary to have a needle biopsy. The sooner it was done the better and I agreed to go that afternoon to get it over with. No point in prolonging the anxiety for any of us.

At a nearby radiology practice, a numbing agent was injected into my groin, presumably to get a sample of the enlarged node. Like everything in this process, it took some time to get the results. When they finally arrived, they reported a very unusual benign anomaly, but not lymphoma. Something called angiomyomatous hamartoma. As my doctor and his registrar delivered the news to us, the girls and I were shocked. We looked at each other, looked at them and wanted so much to share this wonderful moment by yelling out, 'Oh my God!' 'Thank you!' We waited to hear what a lucky day this was, and we should just go home and try and put the whole ordeal behind us. But this was not what these two doctors' faces said. They looked at each other repeatedly, speaking unspoken sentences, none of which appeared joyful.

Finally, they spoke. They said it was a very unusual diagnosis, rarely seen and they were very surprised. We all agreed and said how surprised we were too. It was a miracle. But then, they told us that they would prefer I had a surgical biopsy to make sure. This was an outcome we hadn't expected. Lymphoma or no lymphoma, I thought, but not confusion. I felt angry. I was in no state to make any decisions and I wanted to believe that this benign anomaly was in fact the truth. We'd been through enough. Why should we put ourselves through more angst and fear? I told them I needed time to think about it and they asked me to return in a week to discuss my decision. As soon as we left the room, we sat in the chairs outside the suite. We really did not know how to feel. There certainly was anger. Anger that this just wouldn't end. We couldn't move on whilst this uncertainty hung over us all. It was draining beyond belief. At last we admitted we all felt the same. How can we go on, without confirmation that the nightmare was over? The girls wanted the confidence of knowing for sure. I rang Rick. He too expressed no relief and said it didn't sound right. He felt this anomaly presented differently and he encouraged me to have the surgery. After returning home, we took some time to talk and think it through. After the disappointment and shock had subsided, we decided there really was no other choice than to have the biopsy done. More surgery it seemed, but the extent of it was unknown. Just a groin node sample? A tumour on the spine didn't sound easily accessible. Around my airway? Bloody hell. What a mess.

A week later the girls and I returned and advised the doctors of our decision. They had told us that the groin sample was too ambiguous and would prefer a biopsy of the tumour around my airway. This would require a cardio-thoracic surgeon. We'd all talked about this possibly being the site they would choose, and Elisabeth, who was an ICU nurse, was adamant that she wanted to have a colleague at her work perform the biopsy. This was a different hospital but due to the danger involved, she didn't trust just anyone unknown to her to perform the biopsy. She proposed to my haematologist that this cardio-thoracic surgeon do the surgery. Unusual as this was, he agreed.

*

I was given an appointment with this surgeon quickly due to my circumstances and in just a few days we sat in yet another waiting room, waiting to speak with the man who would hopefully find out once and for all what had set up residence inside my body. Kate, Elisabeth, Philippa and I entered his room en masse, which now makes me smile, as it was to be how we would travel going forward. The surgeon was a serious and gentle elderly man. He had the reputation of operating successfully on very difficult cases. He examined my scan and agreed the only accessible tumour was the one around my airway. He would have to operate close to my aorta and it was quite dangerous. He told me he would do his best to get a sample but said drily that he wasn't going to kill me to get a diagnosis. His words. Sensibly, we all agreed and even were able to muster a smile at his pragmatic common-sense. I understood why Elisabeth wanted me to be in this man's hands.

My surgeon was able to get a sample through the front of my neck.

As was always the case, the results took a while. It was wearing and amplified the anticipatory anxiety of diagnosis and potential treatment. Although not yet diagnosed definitively, I noticed that even a 'perhaps cancer' investigation was beginning to separate me from the lives of those outside this loop. In this way, everything around this disease makes for such a lonely place. Just like I had been prior to my diagnoses, I saw most people being terrified of cancer and loathe to hear about the processes and anxieties that the illness instigates. This further explains why platitudes are so prevalent. Plati-tudes put a full stop to the topic, keeping those who offer them free to shut down any further uncomfortable infor-mation. Understandable. Cancer is frightening.

And so, we waited. And at my desk one day in Novem-ber 2013, the long-awaited results arrived. It surprised me that my surgeon rang me himself. I thought it unusual and it touched me. 'It's definitely some sort of cancer,' he said. He seemed confused by the results; it sounded like he was reading from them as he spoke, but he had said enough. What else was there, really? A result from the needle biopsy had now been refuted and what was feared from two months earlier had finally been confirmed. It was hard news to receive, for all of us, but it at least put an end to the eroding uncertainty. I once again had cancer. It was official. I could now grieve and slowly accept. Not fun, but at least it had some sort of direction, rather than a spinning top going nowhere.

We returned to see my haematologist and his registrar and rather than 'some sort of cancer' as my surgeon had advised, my haematologist told us with confidence that it was Hodgkin lymphoma. He said I would be grateful in time. I had no idea how that made sense. There was a stillness that filled the room after his optimistic predic-tion. So much going on inside for all of us as well as mourning that felt worthy of silence. My doctor was focused on the practicalities and I was unfortunately not able to detect any understanding from him as to how we may be feeling and that we needed a minute. He went on. I was Stage 4. It was explained to me that Stage 4 was tumours above and below the waist plus bone marrow involvement. It all sounded so hopeless. The quiet and stillness remained. The haematologist and his registrar seemed detached and regimented in their instructions, which came next. I was to have a PET scan to confirm the staging of my disease, I was to go to the Day Ward and meet with a nurse and have her explain to me what I would be doing each fortnight for the next nine months. I was then to have a port inserted under my skin above my right breast through which the fortnightly chemo would be delivered. But first I was to have a heart scan and lung scan as some of the drugs to be given could damage these organs and they needed to see if they were healthy enough.

Overwhelm hit. Take a minute. Breathe. As Elisabeth and I had resolved that night, we all needed to take a step back, if only for a day, to digest and calm. Deep breaths, I kept telling myself. Just breathe. *I just need a minute.*

We left the suite feeling lacerated. The painful diagnosis was exacerbated by an overwhelming sense of loneliness. Had we not had each other, this day would have felt very hopeless indeed.

Courage, Please Find Me

I completed all three scans and was told my heart and lungs were well enough to endure the drugs that may affect them, and my PET confirmed Stage 4 disease. That was not easy to hear. I was advised of an appointment to have the port inserted in two days' time. Fear mounted in my body and I tried to manage it with moments of meditation and being mindful of what was happening then and only then, instead of rushing away with all that would come in its own time. But first, I was to meet with the Day Ward nurse to have my orientation. I had to hear what I didn't want to know.

Arriving at the Day Ward, I met with a nurse called Siobhan. As we introduced ourselves I looked around at the many people hooked up to bags of chemicals or blood. Some read magazines, some looked thoughtful, some just slept. None looked like they wanted to be there. Siobhan was a tall, young Irish nurse who was aware of the fact I was newly diagnosed. As I looked at her kind face, I knew my eyes looked sad. I could feel them holding a lot of emotion. I didn't want to be here either, but I had been transplanted here now, walking parallel to my old life. Siobhan talked me through what would be my regimen in the coming months. ABVD was the acronym for the drugs assigned to Hodgkin lymphoma, the B standing for Bleomycin, which had the potential to harm my lungs and the A standing for Adriamycin, which had the potential to harm my heart. My currently healthy heart and healthy lungs – possibly sacrificed for a diseased lymphatic system. How does this make sense?

She went on to explain about fortnightly blood tests, the process of taking my temperature twice a day and the instruction that if I was to develop a fever to go straight to emergency. I felt myself break out in a cold sweat. I think I'm going to faint, I told Siobhan. She lay me down in one of the four beds up against the wall. She told me that it was not unusual for new patients to feel overwhelmed by all the new information and I shouldn't feel embarrassed. I felt I was less embarrassed and more sadly lacking in courage. I felt ashamed. Please, God, help me find the courage I need to kill this disease so I can live, I begged. It was all so much to take in. Nine months of fortnightly treatments was what Stage 4 HL dictated. Eighteen treatments. I had no idea what this would mean for my body and I needed courage so badly. Nurses gowned and gloved in purple with masks over their mouths and protective glasses confirmed my belief that these drugs, whilst supposedly helpful, were also dangerous. Poisons that mandated full body cover for the nurses who administered them. Again, I prayed. *Courage, please find me.* It was in these days that Viktor Frankl's words were introduced to me. I understood that all I had was my response. Everything outside myself had its own governance. All I had was my ability to choose how I was going to make it through. I would contemplate this every step of the way, promising myself authenticity. Orientation over, I went home to once again digest.

*

The morning of the port insertion was a very early start. The nurse put in a cannula the moment I was ushered in and seated, and the doctor came out soon after to explain the procedure. A little sedative to calm me, then a small heart-shaped metal object with three pointed bumps around a rubber circle was shown to me. 'We will create a pocket under your skin and place this object there, and then run a tube up into your jugular vein in your neck,' he said. 'The three prongs help the nurses feel where the rubber circle is so that they know where to insert the needle to attach to the bags of chemotherapy. We will take you in shortly.'

Elisabeth was with me on this morning. We sat quietly waiting and trying to absorb all we had just heard. Finally, they came and wheeled me away on a bed, Elisabeth's eyes sending me messages of strength. The room I entered appeared just like an operating theatre with the doctors gowned up. I was given a little sedative that helped ease my anxiety somewhat and then I was covered from head to toe by a sheet with a hole over my heart and my neck. I felt tugging, and feeding of a tube through my neck, a spill of blood making my neck warm, the doctor asking someone to clean that up and finally the feeling of stitches being inserted over the small metal heart which now resided beneath my skin.

This day was important. It was the beginning of my surrender of my body to others, who I prayed would hold it with honour and gentleness. In every interaction from that day on, I would try to engage with every single person who performed some intrusion into my body on a personal level. I wasn't just the 9am or 2pm or lady admitted with a temperature from ED, but Karina. Karina who was undergoing some difficult stuff. I made a point of engaging with their eyes, smiling and speaking so they could see me. Like how we try and get the attention of the driver's eyes at a pedestrian crossing to ensure they notice us. No different. Can you see me? Can you see the human being before you? When the eyes lock, there is a connection. There is a respect in that. A dignity. So important.

I was wheeled out to Elisabeth and smiled with relief that it was over. 'You okay, Mum?' she asked. Yes baby, all good. The wound above the right breast was about 3.5cm and the one on the right side of my neck 2.5cm. I was a little drowsy and rested for a while outside until I felt more awake, but step one was complete. High five to us both.

All preparatory work having been done, it would be time for the real work to begin in a week or so. I'd made myself a chart on the wall of my kitchen. Eighteen boxes, signifying each fortnightly treatment over the next nine months. I planned to place an 'X' through each, as I completed each chemo session. I wasn't sure how I would feel, but I expected that I would need to feel that this was a road to somewhere, to some day, where it would all be over.

*

I had my first treatment on the 3 December 2013. Kate had moved to Melbourne by this time, but she flew to be with me on the first day and I was so grateful. As I woke on that day, I took an anti-nausea pill an hour before my appointment, as I had been asked. We left the house together and travelled to the hospital in silence. On arrival at the Day Ward, I was greeted with a smile and an introduction and led to a bed. The room was filled with the familiar purple-clad nurses and patients either sitting in chairs connected to a drip or against the wall in a bed. Periodically, a hard case about the size of a small fruit crate would be wheeled in on a dolly. Kate sat beside me as we watched all that went on around us, waiting for what would come next for us. Eventually, a dolly arrived with yet another box and I heard my name. I watched as the nurse unpacked bags of drugs, which I assumed were destined for me. I now understood what was happening.

The nurse approached with a trolley and felt for the three prongs under my skin as I had been told would happen. Then a needle that felt a little like a drawing pin going into a cork board was inserted. It was taped up, so it wouldn't move, and a small bag of steroids was hung, to further assist with nausea I was told. I was then told it was good to drink a lot of water throughout the infusion, so Kate bought me a large bottle. I hate water. I'm constantly being chastised by Elisabeth about my lack of water consumption. I smiled. God has a sense of humour.

Kate had also bought us both the *Daily Telegraph*, which contained the daily crossword. It had always been a link between my father and me. The moments I spent as a little girl, learning at my father's knee how to complete this one specific crossword, became a memory of great love and companionship between us. Kate had adopted this love with me as she grew, and here we sat in silence, sharing what held meaning for both of us, hoping to distract us from the poisons about to enter my body. It seemed to be so counter-intuitive to knowingly have toxins dripping into my body with my consent. Throughout all my years of treatment, my feeling about this would never change.

Finally, the first bag of chemo was hung. We continued doing our crosswords, me stopping periodically to gulp some water. So far so good. I felt okay. After what seemed like about forty minutes, the first bag was done. Next the nurse sat next to me with a fat syringe filled with a red liquid. Kate and I called it the Red Devil. It looked so scary. The nurse sat beside me for the whole infusion, gently pushing this syrupy-looking liquid into me. More water. I asked if I could go to the toilet as my bladder was laboring under the amount of water I was drinking. She said of course, and my drip stand was unplugged from the wall and I wandered down the hall, into the haematology ward to find a toilet. Most everyone I encountered in this hallway, other than the nurses, were bald and had a grey or yellow hue. They, like me, pulled a drip stand on wheels, their eyes looking sunken and dark. I felt such pain witnessing the savagery of their illness and its treatment. As I entered the bathroom, I looked at myself in the mirror. It felt as if I was observing my sad eyes for the first time. I started to sob. I wanted to hug the fifty-five-year-old girl in the mirror. She didn't look like a grown woman with three adult children, but a young girl with the helplessness of a child looking for someone to take care of things and make it all better. How could anyone ever understand the devastation of a cancer diagnosis without experiencing it. The surrender of will to things unimaginable. My heart bled for me, for all the people in the hallway, for those in the Day Ward, for those struck by this illness everywhere else on this planet. I slowly and mindfully wheeled my drip stand over to the toilet, feeling every step as somehow important in the scheme of my life. I sat down feeling vulnerable and uncertain about the future. As I stood, I looked down with defeat at the pink urine the Red Devil had created.

Returning to my bed feeling somber, the remaining two drugs were administered and eventually, at around two-and-a-half hours after arrival, the needle was removed from my chest and I was free to go home. Before I left, I made all my appointments for the following seventeen visits and Kate and I went home. She sat with me for a while. I felt a little odd but okay. Maybe just a little shaky and weary. I eventually told her I was doing fine and insisted she return to her home. She resisted but finally agreed. The other two girls had rung, and I told them also I was fine and not to worry. I made my way to the kitchen to make an 'X' in the first box, and then went to bed.

The Real Journey Begins

It was about 6am the following morning when I sat bolt upright in bed. The nausea and dizziness were overwhelming. I got up and paced, threw cold water on my face, lay on the cold tiled floor in the foetal position, paced some more. Nothing helped. This nausea was powerful and disorienting and made it impossible for me to sit still. I took all the drugs that were suggested, but couldn't find any peace from the nausea. Up and down the hallway I paced for hours. At 9am I rang Elisabeth at the hospital where she was mid-shift. 'Darling, can you help me?' I asked. 'I don't know what to do, I can't find any relief from this nausea'. She said with a worried voice that she was unable to leave work at that moment. I understood. More pacing, crying, ringing the Day Ward. Nobody could suggest anything other than the drugs I had already taken. There was no point ringing anyone else. Elisabeth being a nurse made me think she could help. Silly really when all of the Day Ward was filled with nurses. But to ring anyone else I knew, anyone non-medical, would just worry them and leave them feeling helpless. Elisabeth rang me every hour and nothing seemed to improve. ABVD was usually well tolerated, I had been told. Most people manage to even work while on it. What was going on? I had never felt so ill.

Eventually I heard the front door open and Elisabeth walked in. 'Oh darling, what can I do? I'm dizzy, nauseated and now have ringing in my ears?' She checked my drugs. I had exhausted what I was allowed. From her work in recovery, she said that sometimes people responded to Phenergan when nauseated after anaesthetic. She rang the Day Ward and spoke to them. They didn't believe it would work but it was safe to take. Whilst this nausea was different to any post-anaesthetic nausea I had experienced, I was more than willing to try.

I took a dose. It took some time, but slowly I started to feel things ease. I was able to lie still in bed and finally dozed off to sleep. I slept for quite a few hours and when I woke, I felt groggy, but the nausea was manageable. I was so grateful to Elisabeth. I tried to eat something or at the very least drink something, as I had not ingested anything all day. Water tasted different and even less palatable than usual. I found fizzy water much easier. I ate something small, drank what I could and sat down in the winged chair in my study, just staring into space. How was I ever going to survive this week after week? I was panicked, the nausea still swooshing in my stomach. It felt like travel sickness more than wanting to vomit. *Calm yourself, Karina, take a day at a time. Breathe. Others have survived this and worse.* Just breathe, I thought to myself. Even if I did nothing else but sit in this chair in stillness, time would eventually pass. So, getting myself to and from hospital fortnight after fortnight just had to be mechanical commitment, knowing that with every step, time went by and I was closer to the end. I found comfort in this thought. *This WILL end at some point. I just must find the ability to sustain.* Time would pass 'without my stir', I thought, faintly remembering Macbeth. Just find stillness to sustain, I repeated to myself.

The feeling of nausea never left completely but after day three, I was able to stop the Phenergan, and each day after day five felt a little easier. I felt weak and a little fuzzy so Philippa or Elisabeth would come and walk me up and down the street so I could get some fresh air. The breeze on my skin and face felt wonderful and I enjoyed that so much. After about seven days I started to manage sitting up on the couch and watching some television. The girls would bring meals and help me with my dog and chores, tasks that seemed outside my abilities. By the ten-day mark, I was able to sit at my desk and do some work; enough at least to allow me to keep on top of things. People understood I couldn't do as much as I used to, but I did my best. I limited myself to admin work for my father's property management business, which at least maintained an income for me. My work as a therapist was impossible. My clients deserved a part of me that was no longer there. At least not while cancer took its place. I had momentarily lost the ability to be all about them. Selflessness. Cancer had made me selfish. I don't say this with any shame. How else was it to be? I had to focus on me in order to survive.

*

It was to become clear that I was not one of those who found ABVD easy to tolerate. It bowled me over. Each and every time, I experienced increasing degrees of weakness and frailty. After seeing this, Kate had agreed to fly up each fortnight for my treatments and stay three days to take care of me, so the other girls could work. She would wake me to drink, eat, take medications and would wash my face with cool washers to help me feel human. I slept most of the days she was with me, assisted by the nausea-calming Phenergan. This commitment to my caretaking had made it impossible for her to find work in her new home town. Every fortnight interrupted by days looking after me. I felt guilty. But she continued unwaveringly, every fortnight of treatment from December to July. How hard that must have been for her. Her sacrifice touched me deeply. It was a humbling lesson to need my children as I did. It's not what I wanted, and I found it hard, but life had left me no choice about putting my ego aside and accepting their help, which they offered so lovingly. Still, how does a mother repay her children for such selflessness? It always moves me to tears and I grapple with ways to thank them to this day.

Treatment two had led into Christmas week. I was grateful Christmas was after day ten and I would be able to enjoy it. Rick and his family had arrived from Perth to spend Christmas with all of us. When my brothers and I were all together, it was wonderful. It gave some relief to my girls who desperately needed support, even if it was just someone to hug them and say what a good job they were doing. My twin brothers were older than me by three years, and in the absence of my father, also offered me a place to lay my head when I was feeling low.

We were to have Christmas lunch at my mother's and all the family would be there. It would be the first time I saw my nieces and nephews and sisters-in-law since my diagnosis. I was so looking forward to it and hoping there would be laughter and togetherness.

Christmas morning my three girls and Elisabeth's and Philippa's boyfriends were to come to me for breakfast. As I got up to make some tea and coffee for their arrival, I noticed something tickling my back. I looked behind me and could see nothing, but there it was again, tickling down the centre of my back. I was confused until I caught sight of my pillow. It was covered with a maze of shoulder length brown hair. I reached around to my back and felt more hair. I grabbed it and it filled my hand. I went into the bathroom to look in the mirror. I looked the same. I grabbed my hair into a ponytail with my hand and as I pulled my hand down the ponytail, another handful of hair came with it. I had known this would happen in time and had prepared myself for it both practically and emotionally. I wasn't going to let it spoil Christmas. Gingerly brushing my hair, I pulled it up into a clip and showered. Then I collected the hair on my pillow and flushed it, rinsed my mouth with saline solution and drops to deter mouth ulcers, and set about making the table to welcome my family.

The children arrived. My daughters often ask me when I will stop referring to them as *the children*, particularly as these days they are in their early to late thirties. I suspect never. They are my children and no matter how much I acknowledge and respect their maturity and adulthood intellectually, in my heart they will always be my children. In time they might chat to their therapists about it, I thought to myself that morning, laughing out loud.

We exchanged gifts, laughed and enjoyed being together. I was grateful to feel well and to be able to participate in this Christmas. Watching my girls laugh was amazing. Thank you, God, for these blessings, I thought. We collected the extended family's gifts and headed off for lunch.

We all arrived at my mother's, finding the house and the table decorated so beautifully. The air was thick with the smell of delicious food. Everyone welcomed me with such warmth and caring and it was the happiest I had felt for some time. My work had always taught me that life is never all of anything. There has been such despair and fear, but I needed to try and look for what else was going on at the same time. Sometimes, this was just too hard to see. But on that Christmas Day, amid Stage 4 lymphoma, I had my children and all my family around me and I felt happy.

Transformation

The buzzer rang loudly on my intercom. It was mid-January. I had just farewelled my Cancer Outreach Nurse who had come to take my fortnightly blood and was just tidying up. I looked through my intercom and saw my friend Danielle, who had been my hairdresser for many years. I buzzed her in and as she arrived, we hugged. We had arranged to meet this morning to shave my head. She had a bottle of champagne in her hand. I laughed. She said she had thought I might need some Dutch courage. So sweet.

By now I was losing large clumps of hair and tying it back was no longer possible. I had gone with Elisabeth days earlier to buy some soft caps to cover my head when the colder weather came or even when the sun was strong, so my head didn't burn. I got comfortable in my chair, the gown was placed around me, and the door clicked open with the arrival of Philippa and Elisabeth.

I hadn't asked them to come, not knowing how it would feel for them. Having them there meant a lot.

'Are you ready?' Danielle asked. I nodded. The clippers began moving their way slowly over my scalp, wads of hair falling to the floor. In one way it was a relief, as losing handfuls of hair was distressing and left a trail wherever I went. It was dropping in my food and generally becoming a nuisance. On the other hand, I knew that when I looked in the mirror, I would have started the transformation into what a cancer patient looks like. Up until now, I still had my eyebrows and eyelashes, but I knew this was only a matter of time.

Elisabeth and Philippa joked with me and Dan, trying to lighten the mood. It was a day we would all remember as very different to what we had expected, maybe because we were taking control of the uncontrollable. It felt good to be making the decisions, and that day we did it with as much laughter as we could. When the clippers stopped and Dan brushed the hair from my shoulders and my lap, I looked at my girls with a face that implied, 'Well?' 'It looks great, Mum' they said pretty much in unison. I saw a flicker of sadness in both their faces. I got up and walked to the bathroom to look in the mirror. Bang, my heart hammered. Behind me I saw the two faces of my babies, their eyes telling me they were praying. Praying that I could handle what I saw. I moved my eyes back to my reflection. There I was. Looking at my eyes and my face, remembering my own little-girl face looking not that different. It looked lonely and lost and humbled. Over the coming years, I would often be told that my eyes in treatment looked black and dead. What I saw was different. I always saw young Karina in grief about what had happened to her older self. On this day of the haircut, after the initial shock had subsided, it eventually seemed to hold no weight whether I was bald or not. I clung to the notion that it was not the disease or treatment which had left me without hair that day, but a decision I had made, and that made it okay.

I thanked Dan for making the experience as fun as it could possibly be. She refused to take money no matter how much I argued, leaving after I kissed and hugged her goodbye.

It was cold around my neck with no hair. I realised I would need to always carry a light scarf for warmth; on warm days this would stop the sun burning my neck. Although it was January, my head was also cold, so I donned one of my new caps. It was so soft on my virgin skin. It felt comforting, as if I was nurturing my body, which had been left confused by the new order of things. The girls stayed and chatted for a while. We had a cup of tea, confirming with each other we were all okay and had survived this step. And when we all felt safe in that fact, they went home.

By this time, Philippa and her boyfriend Jorge had found a flat and were living together, so I was glad she was with someone to hug her when times got tough. Elisabeth too had moved in with her boyfriend Nick. I felt such sadness for these young women of mine. They were in newly formed relationships where they would normally be having carefree joy, falling in love, feeling happy – feeling that everything was possible. Instead my girls were caught in this tacky net of illness, unable to separate and just enjoy being in a relationship. The cancer octopus had its arms everywhere.

The Descent

It was a Monday evening in February as I lay in bed. Kate was due in any time. I felt wretched. I had been having trouble breathing and the base of my lungs was sore when I tried to take a deep breath. I had been in hospital in late January with febrile neutropenia, a temperature and low neutrophils, indicating infection. I was kept in isolation on the ward, swinging between feeling freezing cold and melting hot. After days of IV antibiotics and rest, I had recovered enough to go home. However, it had taken its toll and I was feeling weaker than usual, spending a lot of time in bed. I never seemed to pick up and the more I rested the shorter my breathing had become. My breathing would become shallower as I slept; when I woke, there was pain as I would try and breathe more deeply. It felt like the bases of my lungs were deflated and stuck and I could get no air.

When Kate walked in that evening she looked disappointed at me feeling unwell again. I understood. Our times together were increasingly fraught by some complicating illness that would occur over and above the treatment. Facing recurring complication was something that we all had to learn. In regular life when people get sick they suffer for a time and then recover. In my circumstance, there was no recovery of any duration. It was a leap from illness to illness and true relief never came for me or for my family. I apologised to Kate for once again worrying her, which in one sense seemed ludicrous, but also felt apposite. This was painful for us both.

She took me to treatment the following day. The days for crosswords were over. I no longer had the strength or the mental quiet to do more than lie there throughout treatment. Some days I felt well enough to joke with the nurses, others not. On this day I let the nurses on the Day Ward know before beginning the infusions about the pain in my lungs and my difficulty breathing. I had no fever and my neutrophils had recovered enough for treatment, but they thought it prudent to page the registrar, who came and listened to my lungs. 'They are fine,' she said. 'Nice and clear. No reason to withhold treatment.' I felt relieved that it was nothing serious but was concerned that I felt so unwell. Treatment over, Kate looked after me with her usual care and gentleness. However, breathing was difficult and would become more so as the days passed. I would lie in a hot bath, trying to soothe my now aching lungs. As I would lower myself backwards, the water seemed to warm the muscles in my back that were forever straining to give my lungs air.

One day after Kate had already gone home I sat on the couch feeling weak and lacking in oxygen. I tried using Ventolin, as I was an occasional asthmatic. It relieved symptoms marginally. My girlfriend Despina came past with a juice for me. Another friend, Margo, joined her. They both commented that I didn't look that well. I sipped on the juice, hoping to regain some energy, but it seemed to make breathing harder by taking energy away from simply gasping for air. I realised it was getting more and more unlikely that I would feel any better without help from my haematologist. I rang the hospital's specialist suites and they gave me his mobile number.

I had not had a great relationship with my haematologist. As clever as he was, I found him far removed from the humanity and compassion required to serve those afflicted with a disease that had the potential to take their life. I had been contemplating changing doctors for some time, but resisted because it seemed impertinent. This was a denial of my instinct. Since then, I have become certain that I would change doctors again and again until I found someone who held my life respectfully in their hands.

My call to his mobile on this day made concrete my decision to change haematologists at the earliest opportunity. 'Hello, this is Karina Stell, am I disturbing you?' I panted. 'Well, yes. What's wrong?' he said curtly. 'I can barely breathe and I'm not sure what to do,' I puffed again. 'Well can it wait?' he asked, again sounding annoyed. 'I don't think so,' I said. I explained what had happened before my recent treatment and what the registrar had said, and that I had just continued to get worse each day. 'Well go to ED,' he said and hung up.

I could not drive, so Despina took me to the hospital. I could barely stand up to explain to the Emergency clerk why I was there. The triage nurse called me in; she was very kind and could see me struggling. She took me to a bed. I was now heaving for air after the exertion of walking from the car to ED and then the bed. 'She cannot have oxygen. She's on Bleo,' one nurse said. Bleo, as most nurses call Bleomycin, had the potential to cause toxicity of my lungs if oxygen was administered. I was getting so tired from the effort and lay my head on the wheeled tray table crossing my bed. In time, I was taken for a chest x-ray, which looked clear. Doctors listened to my lungs, they sounded clear. I had a CT scan, and finally a result. 'Your scans look very odd, with the appearance of fairy floss within your lungs, but we can't be sure what it is. It looks like some sort of pneumonia,' they said. I could no longer lean back at all. Sitting forward in bed was my only option and I heard this news and prayed they would start to help me recover. I asked Despina if she would let my girls know and if they in turn could inform other family members. She stayed with me until Elisabeth and Philippa arrived and I thanked her so much.

I was taken to the haematology ward and a regimen of every possible antibiotic was hung, injected and orally administered. It seemed constant. Nothing improved over the day or two that followed. One evening I just screamed out, 'Please, I need to see a doctor! I can barely breathe. Please!' After about half an hour, a registrar came from Emergency. He was young and he seemed unperturbed by my emotional state.

'What exactly is wrong?' he asked.

'I have been… lying in this…bed heaving…for air…I am getting worse…every day…and I'm feeling…unable to cope,' I told him, puffing out each phrase. He examined my lungs once again, which he told me were clear.

'All good,' he said. As he was walking away from the ward smiling, he looked back at the nurses' station and I heard him say, 'She's just got herself a little worked up.' I wanted to slap him for the indignity.

I was so afraid and wondered how long this could possibly go on, and how long my heart could take such stress. The lady beside me in bed asked if she could do anything to help me. 'Thank you,' I said. 'I just can't breathe.' It was nice to hear another caring voice besides that of the nurses and my children. I was no longer able to go to the toilet, so a commode was put by my bed by a very sweet nurse who would come during the night and say, 'Any better, Karina?' 'No, I'm sorry,' I would say. The commode was not easy for me. I would look at it, knowing that once I started my journey toward it, my air would become practically absent through exertion. I would make moves in stages, gasping loudly. Finally, I could sit. Once I was finished, the climb back into bed was beyond agonizing. I would reach across to the other side of the bed, all the time gasping, and throw myself on it. I would lie there until I could recover enough to sit up.

Elisabeth had come to be with me one morning, when I was trying to recover from one of these toileting exercises. As I was puffing, trying to settle, my haematologist – I still hadn't managed to find a new one – came to do a ward round. This had been the first time I had seen him since my admission days earlier. He looked at me and laughed as he said, 'Well, you are determined to experience every facet of this illness, aren't you?' I just stared at him and continued to heave. 'We think you may have a nasty fungus which attacks immuno-suppressed patients. It has a long name, pneumocystis jirovecii, PJP for short. We're hoping you don't have it as it can be quite dangerous, but we must find out by doing a bronchoscopy.' I knew what a bronchoscopy was and there was no way I was well enough to endure that kind of invasion. 'We need to get a sample of the fairy floss looking substance in your lung,' he said. Being unlike the usual mucous that is produced in chest infections, this 'fairy floss' was almost impossible to cough up. But if I was to avoid a bronchoscopy, I was going to have to try.

Before he left, Elisabeth asked him if the chest CT from ED had shown any changes in the tumour sizes in my chest. 'Oh, you know, I didn't even think to tell you. Apparently, the nodes are nearly back to normal size.' Elisabeth and I just looked at each other and my eyes bulged with tears. I had no air to cry but the tears rolled down my cheeks and I felt hope. At this announcement he left us and Elisabeth hugged me. I told her how I just had to try and bring something up from my chest. She agreed. She felt as I did: that a bronchoscopy was just too risky with my lungs so limited.

Elisabeth asked my nurse for a specimen jar. I wasn't sure how I was going to do it, but I knew I was going to have to do my best to get something, however small, into that jar. My neighbour in my room had become unwell throughout the day and many medical people came in and out examining her. She had seemed so well that morning, but now she lay in bed motionless and barely able to speak to the doctors. She had some sort of infection, they said. Maybe her line had become infected, they had tried to explain to her. She didn't answer.

I held my specimen jar in my lap, exhausted from days of respiratory exertion. I held it there, knowing I was only going to get one chance at this due to how I would feel after such an effort. The antibiotics continued to be administered despite the fact they seemed to do nothing to improve my freedom to breathe. My neighbour continued to deteriorate and later that evening, the lights were switched on and many doctors entered and told her she would have to go to ICU. She was very ill, and I said a prayer for her as she was wheeled out of the room. What a frightening place this world of illness was.

That night, my specimen jar still in my lap, I felt a small tickle in my chest. I knew they were going to do the bronchoscopy sometime the next day. I had to just try. I coughed hard. Nothing. Grunting for air, I waited to recover. Again. Nothing. And again. This time, a firm piece of something about the size of a large pinhead was in my mouth. I dropped it in the jar and rang my bell. It took some time for someone to come as most of the nurses on the floor were swept up in the emergency confronting my poor neighbour. When the nurse finally came into the room I told her this was all I could do. Did she think it was enough? She didn't think so, but she would send it off. How many days now of this unrelenting deprivation of air, I wondered. I noticed myself thinking of my young self, thinking of my dad and his suffering, thinking I may die.

PJP

The afternoon of the next day brought a flurry of doctors to my room. My haematologist was not with them. The tiny sample I had managed to provide had been enough and showed PJP. No bronchoscopy required. I closed my eyes with relief. They were acting quickly and decisively, and I sensed the urgency of my diagnosis. All other antibiotics were ceased, and Bactrim started. I was to have arterial gases taken to see the percentage of oxygen in my blood, due to some government regulation to do with how starved of oxygen a patient must be before steroids could be administered. What insanity, I thought. If I had had the energy, I would have raged at the stupidity of such rules when commonsense would surely be more compassionate. Could their eyes not see? Why was compliance with an idiotic rule necessary when these medically trained people saw that a patient would benefit from steroids? I once again wearied from seeing the humanity de-prioritized in medicine.

The new antibiotics were hung and the arterial gases taken by a female registrar. I continued to gasp and I was completely exhausted. My back muscles as well as the inner lining of my lungs ached. I'd only slept fitfully since my admission, with my head and pillow still on the tray table as I leant forward. I didn't want any more of my family to come and see me like this. I was afraid how it would affect my mother's health and there was nothing to be gained by her seeing what had already distressed my children so. The irony of being so ill is that you want to spare those you love from the shock of seeing you so distressed. The result is more isolation. It's a psychological nightmare. To this day, I still grieve the horror my father experienced in the grip of cancer. I wanted to spare whoever I could.

The afternoon went by with no improvement. No miracles, even with the correct antibiotic. A male registrar came and sat on the side of my bed.

'No better?' he asked. I shook my head.

'We're quite worried about you,' he said. I knew he meant it kindly, but it made me feel more afraid.

'Please give me steroids,' I puffed. 'I have had them...

over the years…for asthma and…they help so much.'

'Our hands are tied with the government regulations and the blood sample earlier today was corrupted. But I will take another sample and see how we go. I'll be back in a minute.' He left the room. A corrupted sample. Of course it was. Bloody hell. He returned with a kidney dish and took blood from my wrist. He told me he would let me know when the results were back. I wondered how long my heart could hold out.

A female registrar returned after what seemed an eternity and told me the percentage of oxygen in my blood was low and that they would commence steroids immediately. *Thank God!* Within a few hours, air came more freely, I could feel oxygen reaching parts of my body, which had been starved throughout these tortured days. My head became clearer, and I was able to slowly lie back as the stiffness from leaning forward for so long gradually softened. Tears came to my eyes gently as I acknowledged that I would survive. I couldn't wait for my girls to come. I had planned to have a big smile on my face as they approached, telling them all was finally well. As they pulled the curtain back, I did just that.

The Serenity Prayer

The subsequent days brought quick improvement. I was soon well enough to go home, with a plan to skip one chemo treatment giving me enough time to recover. It was a welcome break even though I worried it would give the apparently dwindling cells time to rally. Between a rock and a hard place, I returned home with boxes of drugs to keep PJP at bay for the remainder of my treatment and beyond. I rested gently at home and felt myself strengthen and my head clear enough to think about what I was going to do regarding my haematologist. I knew I had just been through something traumatic and I had felt totally alone throughout the experience in terms of who had me as their focus. I knew this wasn't acceptable and had added terror to an already terrifying episode. My doctor's attitude, whether just a personality idiosyncrasy or a genuine lack of interest, had left me feeling anonymous and irrelevant at a time I needed a strong and compassionate supporter. I was reminded of the Serenity Prayer. It nudged me to act.

'God grant me the serenity to accept the things I cannot change, courage to change the things I can and the wisdom to know the difference.'

There wasn't much I could control, and I'd had to accept so many things. But I needed to have the courage to choose who was going to be my caretaker when I was too ill to take care of myself. I decided I needed to get a new referral from my GP and find myself a new doctor. I was mid-treatment. Not ideal. I was weak and tired, but I knew this was something I had to do. PJP had nearly taken my life. It also left me feeling that I could live or die by the care I received. If living was a real option, then I wanted the best chance. This was not a time for protocol or manners. Could PJP have been raised as a possibility that day they called the registrar before my treatment? I think maybe. I know now that lungs sound clear with PJP, so perhaps this check wasn't sufficient grounds for green-lighting chemo. Particularly knowing that PJP attacks the immune-suppressed, perhaps further investigations could have been made. Could I have been followed up more closely because I felt so unwell? Who knows. But what is most relevant is that I felt that no one 'had me.' That is what really mattered.

I've always believed that emotional survival depends on more than exemplary medicines and techniques. Emotional survival depends on human interactions, and these too must be exemplary. I think I speak for all cancer patients when I say we need to know someone has us cupped in their hands and is watching for every bodily nuance that seems concerning. I'm not worried about hurt feelings or broken procedures in the presence of these kinds of dangers. I am focused on my success at beating a formidable disease and its consequences.

As I had expected, most doctors said they were too busy to take on a new patient. Whether this was true or just a response to my assertive actions, I wasn't to know. But I finally found a female haematologist who was willing to see me through the remainder of my treatment. She was pleasant. Kind. I told her about my experience. I told her I needed more. I was freefalling through a condition and treatment that left me feeling overwhelmed, and I worried I had no safety net. What was the role of my doctor? Surely to be available to me and to guide me through. Could she do that for me? I needed to feel safe. 'Who's got me?' I heard myself say many times through those days. She reassured me that she would be available and that she wanted me to feel safe in her hands. I could only hope.

Her first step was to remove Bleomycin from my regime. My lungs had been damaged and it was too dangerous for this drug to be administered any longer. Further testing showed that my lungs only had the capacity for fifty-seven per cent gas exchange after PJP, with the expectation that this would not improve. So, using Bleomycin further was out of the question. This was scary. Would this change my outcome? As sick as my lungs felt, did I need this drug to destroy every last cancer cell? I was reassured this probably wasn't the case.

And so, the routine continued without Bleomycin. With each fortnight I was willing time to pass. So many days in bed, week after week. So much nausea. It seemed endless. Eventually it was time for me to have a mid-treatment PET scan to see if things were progressing well enough. Unfortunately, this could mean harsher drugs if things were not doing as well as we hoped. For me this would mean a regime called BEACOP. As it's far harsher than ABVD, I wasn't sure how I would manage its side effects. I could only pray that my PET was encouraging. I could feel that my emotional exhaustion was becoming difficult to bounce back from. I felt depressed. Some days I felt limply ill and as my breathing was short, I puffed a lot while walking.

I panted my way into the waiting room the day of my PET. I had the usual anxiety that scans evoked. BEACOP sounded daunting. Today would determine whether this was written for me. As I sat and waited, I noticed a children's playroom just off the waiting room. Children as young as toddlers, with blackened eyes and yellowed complexions, played innocently in this small room. Small tubes entered the noses of some and my heart broke for these little angels. At least I had had a life, I thought. I had married, had children and been given the privilege of watching them grow. These poor little babies had to suffer treatments that must have knocked over their little bodies like a bowling ball knocks down a skittle. How brutally unfair.

My name was called. I was weighed, a cannula was put in my arm and I was taken to a room with a hole in the wall. As I sat in the muted light, I noticed pictures of nature surrounding me. As they fed the tube through the wall, the nurse spoke from outside telling me she was now injecting the radioactive tracer. Painlessly and quickly, she re-entered and removed the cannula, asking me to stay still for the next hour. The gentle landscapes on the walls were presumably there to help me stay calm and relaxed. But an hour gave me too much time to think, so I tried to sleep. When the door re-opened, I was jolted awake.

I was led into a new, very cold, room, which held a large machine. I knew this to be the scanner, having had a PET before. I lay down and I heard the machinery turn on. I made eye contact with one of the technicians.

'Hello,' I said.

'Hello,' came the response. 'Try to relax, this won't take long. Are you comfortable?'

'Yes, thank you.' That quick moment of connection, as always, helped to ease the isolation. The technicians retreated while the scan idled, ready to begin its job of discovery. I heard a door shut behind them and the machine began. As the machine moved back and forth over my body, the moment was emotional and humbling. What are they seeing in that control room, I asked myself. It seemed wrong somehow that they knew and I didn't. I felt small and was filled with anxiety around living or dying. What kind of person had I been in my adult life? Although I was lying on my back, I felt as though I was on my knees, looking to God to bless me with recovery. Would he judge me worthy? What allows one to survive and another to die? This truly was the uncontrollable. So difficult to accept. I felt insignificant and impertinent to think I deserved any more than others. When the technician came in to tell me it was all over I was close to tears. I waited in an adjoining room until she brought me a small disk, which held my future. As was the norm, my report would take a few days.

*

Returning to my doctor days later, I received the positive news that my lymph glands appeared to have returned to almost-normal size. No BEACOP. Thank God! However, my thyroid had lit up, indicating activity of an unknown nature. Was it a cancerous growth or something harmless? I would have to see an endocrinologist. I joked to my brother Rick that he should just tell me which organs are mandatory to keep me alive. Let's just take the rest out, I suggested. He laughed.

I was referred almost immediately and scheduled my appointment for the next Day 10. This doctor was a wonderful young man, who towered over my 1.57m frame. He was gentle and sincere. He looked me straight in the eye as we spoke and listened attentively. He was struck by the dilemma we faced and plainly told me that due to my lung damage, going under anaesthetic was not going to be an easy task. They would have to be very careful. He said that he didn't want to operate twice because of these risks, so if they went in, they would do so with my permission, take the thyroid in full rather than biopsy it to see if it is cancer, then have to operate again if it was. But there was the risk that they would take a perfectly healthy thyroid that merely had a benign growth. I understood, and it was not a difficult choice for me albeit a sad one. The possibility of another healthy organ being sacrificed on the road to survival faced me once more, but my lungs now dictated the choice I had to make. Nothing could be done until I had finished treatment and had regained some strength, so I made an appointment to see him the following January and thanked him as I left.

Day by day I was learning that my cancer diagnosis was not something I could limit to a single part of the body. Cancer of the lungs, kidneys, brain, blood and more, does not always stop there. Organs crumble under the pressure and brutality of treatment. My blood cancer had lead to damaged lungs and perhaps a damaged thyroid. Chemotherapy seemed like a treatment from the Dark Ages at a time when children could be created in a dish. Juxtaposed, this seemed unbelievable.

*

The invasive depression now seemed to be my almost constant visitor and I noticed how hard it had been to maintain hope. There was the illness, there was the treatment and there was the damage from the treatment. This physical thrashing beat down my spirit; hope of ever feeling well again seemed lost. It couldn't just be me who felt this way, I thought. This was part of the whole. It must be the same for at least some others if not all.

Around this time I remembered reading about an American hospital that had placed a bell in the ward, and when patients finished treatment they would ring it.

It seemed that this was something with a lot of meaning, and I asked to speak with the nurse unit manager about donating one. I explained to her what I thought it could offer. Hearing other patients ending treatment and walking away would solidify the idea that this path had an ending. The bell would sound the hope embodied by people moving on from cancer, chemicals and illness, for however long. The nurse unit manager loved the idea and we planned how we would go about it. I would contact a shipyard and order a ship's bell and a plaque, letting patients know that this was the bell they would ring when they finished treatment. I was excited about this gift of hope. Sickness in inexplicable doses was being experienced by most people on this floor, teetering perilously close to death due to any one of the risks associated with lowered immunity. I knew that helplessness and hopelessness had certainly been part of my recent admission. This was something useful to invest my effort into. It mattered and gave my experience with cancer a purpose, even if a minor one.

The End in Sight

Week after week went by, each fortnight waiting for Day 10 where I could be part of the world for a few days. I had always thought that people undergoing chemo became thin and wasted. This idea was validated by what I'd seen in the hallways of the ward. In fact, I had become bloated and unrecognisable. My eyes had sunk into my head, I had no hair on my head or body, my skin was blotchy, and I had gained close to twenty kilos. On some level, I continued to imagine that my appearance hadn't changed; each time I viewed my reflection shocked me. Apparently, my body's response to these drugs was not so strange. Different drugs, different responses. Everyone reacted differently, I was told. This is what the end of treatment was to be for me.

Today was my last treatment. It was late July and only one box remained unchecked in my chart. The bell and plaque had arrived, and I had delivered them to Day

Ward a week earlier. All those months before, sitting in my wing chair, I had known that no matter how I approached it, time would eventually pass, and this would at some point end. And here I was. I didn't feel the elation I thought I would. I was too depleted for that. But I was glad this day had come. One more time, I was waiting on Day 10 to feel vaguely human again, only this time I held the hope that the days thereafter would feel different. Would every second Tuesday come and go and even melt back in as just another weekday? It was hard to imagine.

I was hooked up as usual. I felt I needed to show everyone how happy I was but in reality, I felt sick and sleepy. As usual, drug after drug was administered until we were done. As was the way after the last drug, I felt myself on the outside looking in. In front of me sat a young man with a full head of hair and a healthy-looking face. He was having the process explained to him and I could make out that this was his first treatment day. I wanted to hug him and tell him I knew right down to the pit of my stomach how he was feeling. The sadness, the disorientation and the fear. I watched him as the nurses unhooked me and started their celebratory talk. My eyes were on him whilst trying to sound a part of the celebration. Kate was so excited. I think all my girls were there that day. It feels like a blur. I got up and hugged each of these nurses who had spent every fortnight for nine months caring for me and reassuring me. The bell had not been rung before. I could hear the nurse sitting next to the young man telling him that this will be him one day. The pain I felt for him in that moment. I walked over to the bell and the nurses said, 'Ok, off you go.' I rang it and smiled at all who invested in this moment. My head was spinning, and I felt nauseated. All I wanted to do was lie down and sleep. But maybe down the hall, or in the room, that bell gave others courage and hope that all would be well. I went home to fill in the final box.

*

One of the last processes was my end-of-treatment PET. This held the real essence of what this had all been about. It was hard to feel any relief until this process completed itself, because whilst it went on, I felt like a cancer patient – life had not changed. But as life fulfilled her promise, Day 11 followed Day 10 and slowly, with each passing day, I did feel different. Tuesdays came and went and as hoped, they no longer meant much more than any other day. A month or so passed and soon it was time to see what truth my PET held. Just as before, I would have it at the hospital, feel all the same emotions and smallness, and once again go home and wait.

As my daughters and I sat in my doctor's office the week after the PET, we felt enormous apprehension. The hope, as always, was to hear, 'Everything looks perfect and there is no sign of disease. You're cured.' Of course, in my experience to date, this had NEVER happened. Always there were unanswered questions, hopes that the 'maybes' were not anything to worry about, and a need to talk ourselves into believing it was all good news.

This time was no different. It was possible I had a cancerous growth on my thyroid, my groin nodes on one side were still a little prominent, probably old scarring, but it seemed that there had been a full and total response to the treatment.

Now, it's a little like when your mother asks you if you like her dinner and you say, 'It was absolutely delicious, but I maybe would have liked a little less salt.' All your mother hears is that it was too salty. It's human nature. In this very same way, I heard, 'The nodes in the groin on one side have not gone down totally and the cancer may have spread to the thyroid.' Human nature.

Not wanting to have my concerns bleed across to my children, I came out with the positive notion that I had been cured apart from the issue of my thyroid, which we would address the following January. Being a nurse, Elisabeth may not have bought my bullshit, but like always, we all left squashing our questions and trying to focus on the phrase that there had been 'a full and total response to treatment.' We ignored the words 'it seemed that.'

I knew unless I had a zipper down my front and the doctors could examine my insides under a microscope, this was the best they could say with honesty. But as a cancer patient, 'maybes' and 'seems' never feel safe. Still, we spread the news amongst the family and closest friends, and everyone felt huge relief. I was so happy that for them at least, it felt over.

*

Before we all faced January's surgery, there were a couple of things I needed to attend to. The first was to buy two wedding dresses. Both Elisabeth and Philippa became engaged straight after my PET. Their partners were both wonderful men, whom I loved. I couldn't have been happier. It was amazing that we found ourselves in this place of so much joy and celebration after what seemed like an eternal dark tunnel. Two weddings to organise was an experience beyond fun, especially since these were days I hadn't been sure I would see.

Second on my list was to see my gynaecologist. I had not had any checkups for my vulvar cancer whilst undergoing lymphoma treatment, as I was just too unwell to tolerate colposcopies or to have biopsies while my platelets were low.

My gynecologist was a special woman who had always been very dear to me. We talked woman to woman and she had taken a real interest in all that had happened to me. She too felt that my poor immunity had led to the cancers I had experienced. I had been told by my haematologist that ABVD can create secondary cancers over time. Because I had had a gynaecological cancer, this was concerning to me. I had witnessed a friend lose her life to ovarian cancer and I knew it was notoriously hard to recognise in time. I asked my gynaecologist how she felt about removing my ovaries, my last remaining gynecological organ, at the same time as my endocrinologist removed my thyroid, to avoid two anaesthetics. She said she would liaise with him and see if it was possible. These two very special people spoke and agreed to operate in the same theatre session. Sharing an operating theatre was not common, rare as far as I understood. But their agreement to do so reduced the risk to my lungs. I felt so grateful to both of them for putting ego aside for my benefit.

*

The day of surgery my lungs were sore. The anaesthetist was at pains to make sure he kept me as safe as possible. My first surgery was to be the removal of my thyroid. The cut was to be in the same spot that my biopsy was taken from all those months ago to determine if I had lymphoma. My doctor joked that he could do a neater scar than the cardio-thoracic surgeon had. I smiled. Then while I was still under anaesthetic, my ovaries were removed. Neither of these organs showed signs of cancer. The surgeons found a benign growth on my thyroid and my ovaries without any pathology. The fact of no cancer put balm on the news that I had lost a healthy organ.

I woke in the High Dependency Unit, everyone fearing how my lungs would cope. Apparently, they did very well. My chest rattled quite a bit as I coughed but there was no issue with getting air. All that could be done had been done to protect me. Now it was just a matter of healing.

After a few days in hospital, I went home to recuperate. The girls would come and go, as would friends and family. All surgeries were completed and constant venous access was no longer required, after more than a year. My port removal was next. I would see my haematologist to arrange this, then there would be a meeting with a new doctor who would take over my after-care. She was very pleasant, but I felt less invested when I met her, as I was emotionally spent with regard to doctors and hospitals. I would see her monthly after my port removal to keep an eye on my recovery and monitor for relapse. But for now, I needed to focus on weddings and my girls.

Blessings

So, two weddings a month apart. There was so much to do. Wedding protocols were now less about perfection and more about each couple being able to celebrate in their own individual way that held meaning for them. I enjoyed watching them all find what made them happy. They deserved it all. They had given up a lot for the sake of cancer. Now it was their time to fulfill some dreams of their own. As we chose dresses, stylists and venues, there was not one argument. Not one wish for more or better. Everything was enough. Everything was a blessing. We all had learned what to focus on. It was a lesson treatment had taught us. What did we value in life? Life went up, down and all around and being able to pluck out what really mattered was a gift that cancer gave us.

*

One evening as Elisabeth and I sat talking about the storm we had all weathered, I was sharing with her a memory that was prompted by how happy I now felt. As a young girl, I remember being in trouble from my father for disobeying him. In my memory, I was crying. We were in the front garden. I felt miserable. It always hurt so much when he was unhappy with me. I noticed another young girl about my age walk past with her father, beach towel and ice creams in their hands. Even so young, I learned a life truth that would endure: my best days could be someone's worst, and my worst, someone's best. As Elisabeth and I sat together, I thought about our day of shock and diagnosis, and how it had seemed inconceivable that life outside continued seamlessly when the clock seemed to have stopped for us. On my daughters' wedding days, it was important to me that those facing their shock of diagnosis would be remembered in the yin and yang of life, that their pain mattered on the day we were all feeling such joy.

We had all been changed. It was hard for me to let go of that world. And knowing now that it had always run parallel to my life before I fell ill made it hard to forget those suffering just because we had moved on. As I shared with Elisabeth this childhood memory and discussed my feelings and what I had learned from it, I could see she wanted to leave it behind. It was too hard. We'd done our time. Not that she could ever forget, even though she would like to. I understood. I conceded it had changed each of us differently.

Wanting to change the subject, I asked her if she had any news. She had a half-smile on her face and just kept staring at me. 'What?' I said. No answer. I started to suspect what I hoped was true as she looked so excited. 'No!' I said as she started to smile wider. She nodded her head and I just couldn't believe we could be so lucky. Nick arrived shortly after and I'd never seen them so happy. The joy at the notion of their growing a family was deep, meaningfully underscored by our earlier conversation. No wonder she had not wanted to think about cancer and its lessons. She had the excitement of something new and wonderful that could stomp out the memories of the last years. I totally understood and wanted nothing less for her. After the elation, however, I stopped for a moment and quietly remembered those who just heard something much more jolting.

Circa 1980: Karina with her beloved father, George.

Late 1960's: Karina in primary school.

Circa 1989: Karina with her three girls, (from left) Kate, Philippa and Elisabeth.

2004: Karina with her sisters-in-law (from left) Bronwyn and Helen.

2007: Karina with her brother, Dean.

2007: Karina with her brother, Rick, on a family trip to Greece.

2011: Karina with her eldest daughter, Kate.

September 2011: Karina with Philippa and her mother Katherine, at Philippa's farewell to London.

2012: Karina with her cherished dog, Annabel.

December 2013: Karina and her twin brothers (from left) Rick and Dean. This was over the Christmas period after commencing her chemotherapy for Hodgkin Lymphoma.

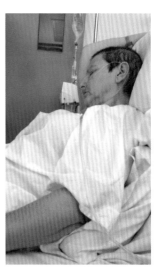

February 2014: During Karina's admission to hospital for PJP.

April 2015: Karina walking her daughter, Elisabeth, down the aisle.

April 2015: Karina with one of her closest friends, Despina.

May 2015: Karina and Philippa, dancing to their song, 'Brown Eyed Girl' at Philippa's wedding.

December, 2016: (From left) Elisabeth, Philippa, Kate and Karina - Christmas in Perth during Stem Cell Transplant.

December 2016: A small respite from nausea during Stem Cell Transplant.

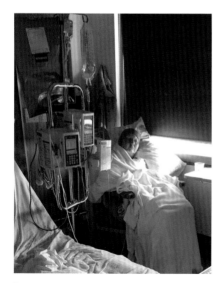

January 2017: Immediately post Stem Cell Transplant - Karina became very ill.

April 2017: Post Stem Cell Transplant. Karina with the bell she donated to the haematology ward in 2014. It was later named 'The Stell Bell' and now sits mounted in the Nelune Cancer Centre in Randwick.

August 2017: Pictured in back row from left, Rick, Karina and Dean with their mother, Katherine, at her 90th birthday celebrations

March 2018: With three more of her closest friends (from left), Michele, Jenny and Kathy.

June 2018: Captured by Karina's three year old grandson, Jack whilst on a weekend away in the Blue Mountains - a few days prior to Karina's stroke.

July 2018 (during palliation)**:** From left, Jorge, Kate, Nick, Elisabeth, Karina & Philippa, at one of Karina's favourite restaurants, Aria.

Hello... Is Anyone Listening?

Driving home the following afternoon after a wedding dress fitting with Philippa, I felt my thigh start to sting as if I had been bitten by a mosquito or small spider. As itchy as it was, it was also painful. When I tried to gain some relief scratching through my jeans, I felt the heat coming from it. I hoped I hadn't been bitten by anything venomous. By the time I got home, it was driving me crazy. I pulled down my jeans and saw a welt the size of a five-cent coin on my upper thigh with a red circle of about six inches surrounding it. It certainly looked like something had bitten me, so I put on some antiseptic cream with lignocaine, hoping it would ease the itch. I sat back and relaxed, having my dinner in front of the television, trying to ignore the partly numbed irritation on my leg.

During the night, however, the itch became worse and seemed to spread all over my body. When I woke the next morning, my arms were covered with a rash that looked like chicken pox. So too my torso, front and back. Visiting my GP, she assured me it wasn't chicken pox and I was given a referral to a dermatologist. The rash was biopsied, and, in a few days, I was advised it was something called 'granny anny', or granuloma annulare, an innocuous rash sometimes indicating thyroid illness or diabetes.

Later that week I went to see my endocrinologist and was told that all levels from synthetic thyroxine were normal, and the rash would not be associated with the thyroid. As I did not have diabetes I was sent to an immunologist. Blood tests showed something called an IgG deficiency – perhaps this was the cause of the rash? And so, I had several IgG infusions, which did not seem to make any difference. Each specialist visit involved booking in, taking blood, getting results, receiving treat-ment. Being hawked from doctor to doctor was doing little to ease my rash or my fear and as the weeks started to turn into months I got increasingly tired and frustrated.

I continued to prepare for the girls' weddings whilst at times being sent mad by the itch. This rash was not the first sign that something was amiss. I was depressed at still feeling unwell and my feet and hands were swollen constantly. My haematologist perceived my mood to be an inability to cope with post-cancer wellness and anxiety. She introduced me to a support nurse who offered many arms of help on behalf of the hospital. However, as I felt unwell and at the tail-end of treatment, this was not what I expected. On several occasions, I had said to the haematologist, 'If this is what it is after nine months of chemo, I'm happy to accept this as my future, but I need some guidance as to whether this is what is normal to experience.'

Whilst the doctor appeared compassionate when listening to me, answers never came, and I gleaned very little from each visit other than the fact of my blood tests being good. According to her metrics, I was doing well. When a patient's experience is different to a doctor's opinion, there seems nowhere to go in spite of the certainty that something is not right. Perhaps it was my failure to be forthright about what I needed. I felt I was asking, but maybe it wasn't enough. Then again, I had not had nine months of chemo before, and if this was the legacy of such treatment, how would I know? All I wanted was for someone to tell me. Instead, I was continuing to shut up and accept that this was how I might feel from now on.

Things changed however, with the persistence of the rash. After many months, it couldn't be ignored. It was visible evidence of the illness I had been feeling. I told my doctor that I had seen many lymphoma message boards with posts about people suffering with a rash that wouldn't go away. Others would complain of itching and no rash but would write they were just as uncomfortable. She knitted her brow as if she had not heard of it before. I repeated that this had been reported on lymphoma websites specifically. No connection. I was left lost.

And so, in early 2015 I was sent to another dermatologist who biopsied the rash once more. Once from under the arm and once from my back. The samples were sent to the Peter McCallum Cancer Institute which after some time reported that they had found very unusual and 'atypical' results. It certainly wasn't 'granny anny'. They weren't sure how I had received that diagnosis previously, and the institute asked to see the earlier slides. Here we go again, I thought. They found that, as in the earlier slides, T lymphocytes were present in abundance, but reports were inconclusive. The report did state that the biopsies would require 'careful clinical correlation with the overall dermatological and haematological findings and in particular the previous history of lymphoma'. Still no connection. At the foot of the report there was a post script stating that the pathologists had found this case very interesting and would like to be informed of the outcome. Them and me both. I was then asked to attend a day where I would sit in a room whilst dermatologists went from room to room to look at 'interesting' cases.

The day was an awkward experience, with doctors entering making 'hmmm' noises and leaving. For me, there was no value in this and I began to feel angry. How many doctors had to see me before someone recognised what was happening? I was despairing.

Every morning I was waking up with a sensitivity in my skin, though it was not intolerable. I would have a cool shower and I put on oversized clothing so there was not too much contact against my skin, as it could start the cycle off if too tight. In this way the days were not too difficult. But invariably something changed from late afternoon; the itching would start and continue for hours.

I began to have itching on my feet, including the soles,

as well as my hands. It made sleeping at night difficult. Sometimes the rash would not appear, but this did nothing to change the intensity of the stinging and discomfort. It became so intolerable that even though it was the heart of winter I would have to plunge my hands and feet into cold bath water to get some relief. In the peak of irritation, they would swell, and the skin would feel tight. I was unable to use my hands at all whilst in this state as they felt like the skin was cracked and burnt. The morning after these episodes, I would see bruising under the skin where there had been itching the evening before. I could no longer have hot baths or showers as it would start the sequence off ferociously.

My haematologist was at a loss (despite my insistence that I believed this was related to lymphoma and my request to be scanned) and decided instead, to send me to a neurologist to investigate the possibility of neuropathy after treatment. This didn't make sense to me. Whilst I knew I had some nerve damage in my feet, this was an itch, not nerve pain or numbness.

Whilst all these investigations were going on and I was going to specialist after specialist, I would continue to read posts by lymphoma patients suffering as I was.

Again, I raised this with my haematologist as a possibility but was told it had nothing to do with lymphoma. In the meantime, the dermatologist had arranged for me to go three times a week to a UV light booth to help with the itching. It did little to help. I was diagnosed large doses of antihistamines, none of which did anything.

Distressed, I would go to bed each night with stinging in my legs, arms and my right shoulder, which would bring me to tears. My toes would be so itchy that I would gouge at them. My immunologist suggested that on unbearable days, I could take high doses of dexamethasone, (steroids) to help. I was only to take them for three days, but he felt it may help. After my first dose, I noticed a difference. By day three, at last a reprieve. I felt human again. I could sit still and not be tormented by these incessant symptoms.

This relief would last for about a week, and then slowly the symptoms returned. My torso and arms were covered with a mat of raised rash. I was wondering how I was going to put anything next to my skin that looked mildly acceptable at Elisabeth's wedding as the dress I had bought was lace and I wasn't sure my skin could take it. My feet would sting in shoes. The timing was awful.

This wasn't about vanity, but about how I was going to walk my daughter down the aisle in this condition.

The day before the wedding I took the dexamethasone. Blessedly, relief came. I was grateful I was able to be a part of things, and even though my skin felt sensitive and tender, I was able to enjoy one of the most important days in her life. I was able to speak about how much I loved her and how proud of her I was. This was the day that these feelings should be shared, and I thanked God I was able to concentrate and let her know. With the help of steroids, my head was clear, and I was able to take it all in.

After the wedding, I went to see the neurologist. I told him that I was concerned this was lymphoma. He said that I had no evidence to base this on and referred me on for some nerve conduction studies. These showed some loss of sensation in my lower legs and feet, but I knew this had nothing to do with any other symptoms I was experiencing.

On Philippa's wedding day a month later, my legs and feet were, if possible, even more swollen. My body was covered in rash and my dress rubbed against the stinging skin, causing me to feel distracted and depressed. I had taken a lot of dexamethasone over the month despite being warned that it should be an occasional fix. I would have to just manage without it for a while. I was determined to focus on the day, as there were no second chances. It was hard, but I watched and celebrated with my baby girl and her new husband. I wish I could have given it more of me, but the physical sensations were just too overwhelming. Hopefully no one noticed. Once again, I read my speech, letting her know how proud her mother was. I danced with her to Van Morrison's 'Brown Eyed Girl', which was always my song for her, and I watched her looking so beautiful and happy. Being there for my daughters was now something I did not take for granted. Every moment, they all needed to know their mother was proud and loved them without parallel. My father had gone, but in his time here he always let me know what I meant to him. Throughout my life, I have continued to hold those memories so tightly and they keep him with me. Throughout their lives, but especially on their wedding days, I wanted to give my girls the same.

*

Months and months of the same daily and nightly routines continued. The rash was now disappearing most days, but the itch remained, just as savage. Night times were still unbearable. Life had to go on. In between doctors, I still had to work. I told my Immunologist about my fears surrounding the rash. He just looked at me and said, 'If the lymphoma comes back, you'll just treat it again.' So easy to say when you don't really understand what that means in a *lived* sense, I thought. It was around this time something in me gave up. I couldn't argue any longer. So, I would have a rash for the rest of my life, there would be no solution and if it was lymphoma, it would make its presence felt eventually in a manner that my doctors acknowledged. I was out of energy. I decided there was no point in seeing any of these specialists any longer and would just have my monthly visits to my haematologist. My depression was deepening, but I did my best to keep living as normally as possible. The neurologist scheduled more tests, looking for further answers. I never went.

*

The light in this year was the birth of my first grandchild. A little angel boy named Jack. Delicate and tiny, he was born in September 2015. And then a second grandchild came in June 2016, a little baby girl to Philippa and Jorge. Beautiful Chloe. She was just gorgeous. The daytime easing of symptoms allowed me to enjoy these little babies. And even though I didn't really have the stamina to babysit for any length of time, I helped as much as I could.

By September 2016 I thought I would lose my mind. There was no quality of life. I was always distracted by stinging, bloating and exhaustion from lack of sleep. In the end, my haematologist, in seeming exasperation, decided to give me a PET. She was, she said, trying to put my mind at ease. I was unable to shake the belief that this had something to do with lymphoma.

A Rash Isn't Just a Rash

Another PET was not something I relished. I knew they had the potential to cause cancer themselves when done too often. But if this was going to be the only way to exclude the possibility of lymphoma, I had no choice. I was so depleted by the constant illness and even more by surrendering to what will be, depression tiring me more than anything else. Believe me, being proven right was not something I wanted. I knew the statistics. The incidence of relapse within eighteen months gave a very poor prognosis. But how could lymphoma patients be writing endlessly about an itch like mine and yet every doctor I speak to look puzzled at the suggestion? What I did know, was that if no answers lay in this PET, I was going to have to ask my GP to refer me to palliative care to control the symptoms of this unknown intruder.

As always, PET results would dictate my future. As I lay in the scanner, I prayed it wasn't lymphoma. I wanted to hear those words, to just leave this fear behind. This was the first step to that end and I was terrified. As I left the hospital after the PET, I remembered Julius Caesar – 'the die is cast.' Whatever was, was. I would just have to wait. It was now the end of September 2016. Two years and two months since the end of chemotherapy. I had had this rash since February. I prayed, *not again*.

*

My doctor rang to make an appointment to discuss the results. How cancer patients place one foot in front of another sometimes baffles me. To walk myself into her room, when I wanted to run in the opposite direction, felt like dragging lead boots. She asked me to sit and said, 'This is the reason I didn't want to scan you. There are two enlarged nodes in your groin, one on each side and some enlargement in your armpits. It's probably nothing but now we have scanned you we have to investigate. This is what I try to avoid.' I got the impression she was telling me that I had launched some unnecessary sequence that was a waste of time, causing everyone to worry.

I'm not the doctor here, I thought. Tell me why my

skin is reacting as if it is being relentlessly provoked and we can walk away from these results. But in the meantime, whilst we had no answers, what was I supposed to do? I felt I wasn't being a 'good patient.' I was being bothersome, as though the doctors were saying, 'We've told you it's not lymphoma, and now we have to sort this out.' I was wedged inside the clash of humanity and intellect.

A week later, I sat with Elisabeth in the waiting room of the public hospital day surgery. The same doctor who removed my thyroid was going to take a sample of the largest node, which was in my left groin. How many waiting rooms had we sat in? How much adrenalin had pumped throughout our bodies, time and time again? Each and every member of my family, no one had escaped. Seven years on from my first seemingly simple diagnosis, we still all rode this rollercoaster. We had all become so wearied.

Light sedation was used due to my lung issues. So light in fact that I woke at one point in the procedure saying, 'Ouch.' I think I shocked the medical team. Then I heard someone say, 'Don't worry, you won't remember.' But I did. It made me smile when I relayed the story to Elisabeth later. It's probably not often that the patient pops their head up to comment during an operation. I woke from the sedation with my body on fire with itching. I also felt nauseated. 'Phenergan please,' I whispered softly to the nurses. 'Phenergan is all that works.' Thankfully I didn't have to argue as they knew it would help the stinging itch. Relief came from both the nausea and the itch and I relaxed.

I was given dressings to take home. The wound was not overly uncomfortable, but the painful part was yet to come. Waiting two weeks for a result, I kept ringing my doctor to find out what was taking so long. She wasn't sure. She'd been chasing it up. Then she rang me to just come in for a chat whilst we waited. This seemed strange. What was there to chat about if no results were through? Still, I agreed to go and with my heart in my mouth, I waited in the cancer and haematology outpatient waiting room for her to call me in. I felt sick. My body was shaking. When I walked in, I attempted a smile and watched her closely to see for any unusual behaviour. She sat facing me. Recalling it now, I remember the conversation as if it were yesterday. She told me how shocked she was. She told me the pathologist had taken so long because it was such a difficult sample to read. She said on Friday afternoon of the second week, he had gone home still not being able to write a report. But then on Monday, 'He called it. He said it was a relapse of Hodgkin Lymphoma.' She told me how sorry she was.

In all my diagnoses, I had never felt like I did in that moment. To this day, I don't think I have fully recovered. I could physically feel my heart breaking. Such grief in my chest. I bowed my head and said, 'Oh God.' I sobbed and sobbed. I felt like I was going to vomit and wanted to just lie on the floor. 'I can't believe it,' she said as I looked at her, my eyes streaming with tears. 'I told you,' I said softly. 'No one would listen.' Silence. I continued. 'Oh no, I've just met my grandchildren. They won't remember me.' More sobbing. Agony like I've never felt before. It was like a hot blade cutting right through me. 'I can't go through that all again, my body can't take it. I'll die from treatment,' I said.

I asked her how long I would have without any treatment. She replied that it was hard to say but probably up to a year. Again the agony, my body squeezing out more and more tears. I felt myself wailing from the pit of my being. Eventually I got up to go. She asked me to go home and just digest the news. Then I could come back and discuss the options available. I walked out feeling like the hall could swallow me and I would never be seen again.

I messaged a colleague as I walked with no real purpose. 'It's back,' I wrote, 'I need to hide away and think things through. I won't be back to work for some time.' I reached the elevator and tried to calm my breathing. My mind was racing at a hundred miles an hour. I rang my brother Dean. 'It's back, Dean. I told them. Nobody listened…I can't do it, I can't. It's too much to ask of someone. I feel I can't trust anyone. That's just how I feel. I'll go into treatment again and I'll die.' We cried together.

I was on my way to Elisabeth's home, where she and Philippa waited. As I was walking up her steps, Rick rang.

'I heard,' he said.

'I can't, Rick. No more. I can't take any more.'

'Only you can decide what's next. They will probably want to do a stem cell transplant. It's a dangerous business. There is a mortality rate of about five per cent,' he replied. I just shook and listened to him. 'It'll be up to you, but it won't be easy. There's about a forty per cent success rate,' he said softly.

'I think I'm going to faint,' I said. 'I love you, but I have to go.'

I walked up the stairs to my daughter's unit, my face telling everything my family needed to know. I tried so hard to hold myself together, but I just couldn't. I repeated to them both, 'I can't, I just can't.' They comforted me, putting their arms around me, ignoring their own broken hearts. 'It's okay, Mum, we'll support whatever you want to do.' I looked at my grandchildren, just little babies. They would hear about me, but I reached in my heart for some way to help them remember me touching them, holding them and loving them. I rang Kate and once again broke her heart. Then I went home to grieve. But before I let myself enter into the fullness of grief, the words 'he called it' rang in my ears. Called it? This was my life we were talking about. I emailed my haematologist and told her I wanted a second opinion.

A Dying Spirit

It was now late. I got in my car to drive home but found myself driving toward my brother's house. I was in such pain I didn't know what I was doing. I rang his doorbell and he opened the door, his face grey. I leaned into his open arms and became limp. I wailed from my core. I felt my sister-in-law's arms also encircle me. There was nothing to say.

My mother, who was now eighty-nine, had moved in with Dean and Helen, and as I made my way down the hallway, I saw her face. How many times was I going to do this to her? She held me and just said how sorry she was.

I sat there for a good hour, surrounded by the two elder members of my family, dreading the possibility that they wanted me to do something I couldn't. In fact, it was exactly the opposite. They told me that they would support whatever decision I made. They loved me enough to let me choose. I felt safe here, and I knew that I would return to this house often to feel that safety and love, over and over.

I went home eventually, having asked Despina to update our other friends; I had nothing to give. Then I lay in bed like a frightened little girl at death's door. A blessing I have always had is that when I am upset, my body copes by sleeping. Thankfully sleep came. I turned my phone off for the night, needing this time to come to terms with what I was facing and to seek my God to comfort me.

I woke suddenly in the night, gasping for air. I started weeping loudly. It wasn't enough to relieve what was going on inside me. A panic attack. I had had them before. My heart banged hard against my ribs and my legs felt like they were on fire. *Dear God, someone help heal this agony.* I wanted to run from my bed and leap over my balcony. *I can't face what lies ahead. I just can't. I have no way out...no way out.* I started weeping again, pleading with God to take me in my sleep. Finally, exhaustion came, and I closed my eyes.

*

The days ahead felt no different, with this cycle of anguish faithfully repeating itself over and over. Amidst such terror, I had to face some daunting tasks. Several months earlier I had bought a new unit off the plan in Botany to house my growing family. If I had no treatment, I would not live to see it completed. I had to ring the saleswoman and ask her a big question: if the second opinion confirmed my diagnosis, would she resell it on to someone else, so I didn't leave my children with problems? She was incredibly compassionate and said they would do what they could.

In addition, I had to message clients and let them know I was taking sick leave and gently move them on to my dear colleague Michael in order to stop them feeling abandoned. I had to sign out of our business's social media, as I was the one who entered messages each day, messages meant to inspire and comfort. I had worked hard to build my practice. Now this held no meaning. And I had to meet with my lawyer and make sure my will was up to date and easy for my children to access.

Given the state I was in, these were excruciating tasks. I felt like I was trying to swallow a refrigerator each time I attempted to complete a job. Once done, I would return to my grief and sleep, and my children and family, who were my main solace.

As I was crossing items off the To Do list, my children were aggressively palming through different non-invasive solutions. Green smoothies, organic vegetable-only diets, sites where people had supposedly cured cancer by eating different combinations of foods. I stopped drinking diet soft drinks, eating meat, sugar or anything with preservatives. I ate only organic food in the hope that the poisons that had supposedly been ingested by me and maybe kept causing my body to make cancer cells could be reversed. I suspected this wasn't effective, at least not for me, however it gave my children hope and I continued to try for their sake. This was their only way to take some sort of control as we waited for the second opinion.

Meanwhile, I swung between panic attacks and sleep. The chance to lie down and escape in sleep was all I worked toward each day. At night when panic would strike, Elisabeth would come, and we would walk arm in arm through the nearby Westfield, around and around until I exhausted myself. Walking seemed to forestall the need to take Valium, which Rick had prescribed to help with the panic attacks. Managing these and the continuing itch and all its gifts, my connection to life felt no stronger than a piece of thread.

*

Within a few weeks of my rediagnosis, my doctor asked to see my girls and I. She wanted to explain some of the options that lay ahead. We arrived together with the babies. We felt like this was a black day. We listened to her suggestion that I have an autologous stem cell transplant, in other words, using my own stem cells. I was told, as Rick had warned me, it was dangerous. If I managed to come out of the other side of treatment, it would increase my chance of survival to forty per cent. I asked to be put on a drug trial. I was told I had to have had a failed stem cell transplant to be eligible. I asked for the same treatment as I'd had before – at least the risks seemed less. They were not prepared to give me this treatment again. In fact, they were not prepared to discuss any alternatives (including immunotherapy – which whilst not curative, was certainly a potential treatment option I would later learn about under the care of Dr Joske). But for now, I was told if I did nothing –

perhaps a year. We left the room distraught.

We sat in the gardens in the front of the hospital to just digest. I said to my girls that things didn't look very hopeful. They agreed. We sat quietly and solemnly together, lost in our feelings.

*

Often, when problems circle my head, I sleep to escape. When I wake, my mind has plucked some truths about what is going on. It's a gift I rely on and also the reason I don't push myself to make decisions consciously; I know eventually my sleep will sift through it. A few afternoons after our visit to the doctor, I woke after such a nap. The words came: 'What really scares you about having more treatment? Other than death, Karina, what are you really afraid of? The essence of what was going on lay in this one question. The answer came quickly. *I don't trust my medical team.* Clarity. *I don't trust them with my life.*

Had anyone else ever felt this way through treatment? I'm sure they must have. Not all relationships between doctors and their patients are fairy tales. I had to say the truth as it was for me. And this was it.

Before I could think on it further, I found myself dialing Rick's number. I talked to him about what I had just unearthed in myself. 'If I come to Perth, will you be my advocate? Once they inject those poisons into my veins, I lose the ability to care for myself, especially with the extreme nausea I experience. I can't advocate for myself. Will you be my advocate?'

'Of course, but in reality, your doctor should be your advocate.' Emotion swallowed me. I had not felt this once since my lymphoma diagnosis. Maybe my panic attacks were God's way of alerting me to the fact that I needed to find another path.

'Leave it with me as I have an idea of someone, but coming over here will be a big thing and how will you manage?' Rick said.

'I'm not sure, but I'll know when I get the right doctor,' I replied.

Shortly after, Rick called me back and gave me the name of a Professor David Joske, head of haematology at Sir Charles Gairdner hospital in Perth. He said he was willing to see me and to my surprise, within half an hour I had an email from him in my inbox. He said he would be happy to see me and asked if I could arrange for my slides to be forwarded to his lab for investigation. I said I would advise my haematologist of his request straight away and would copy him in. Suddenly I felt hope.

I googled him. I found his TED Talk on bringing humanity to healthcare. I listened in disbelief. All that I had lacked until now was in his description of the doctor–patient relationship. My hope grew. I read a quote of his:

'What has really shaped and defined and given meaning to my life is doctoring, and I'm old fashioned enough to think of doctoring as a privilege and a calling.'

I immediately emailed my haematologist and copied Prof Joske in. I asked for my slides to be sent to him at the address he had given. She wrote back confirming that she understood I was seeking another opinion and that she would send the slides as soon as possible. The second lab had still not returned with a diagnosis, leading me to believe that there was something unusual about these slides. I completed all the formalities with Sir Charles Gairdner in order to gain a physical appointment and was told until the slides arrived, it was best to wait.

I rang my children. I told them what had occurred in the past hour or so. That I felt hope. My diagnosis had not changed but I had. I'd figured out what was destroying me inside. I named my fear. I knew there was now another way.

My girls arrived and we talked and talked. They couldn't believe the change in me. I wasn't sure why it was so dramatic either, but feelings just are. I had believed it to be so impermissible to say that I didn't feel safe with my doctor (and in fact the whole department) that I had swallowed these feelings. For a brief and terrible moment, I had chosen to let myself die rather than let them care for my illness.

The crucial thing about my realization was that it was not based on any medical or professional foundation. It had to do with human relationships. At times, being a cancer patient has felt like a stripping away of the right to say, 'No! I don't want that!' 'I don't feel safe with you!' But it would take my third diagnosis to realise that I could speak up for my life, even if I was scared of hurting someone's feelings or offending a protocol. If not then, when would be a more fitting time?

A Game Changer

My slides eventually made their way to Western Australia and to Prof Joske's lab. I was contacted by his outpatients' department and was given an appointment in October. Kate and I flew across the country, anxious to meet this doctor whose public persona had given us the hope that he was meant to be my doctor. We checked in to our hotel and spent the remainder of the day resting. Lymphoma is tiring. It takes very little to become exhausted. It was helpful to have that time as my appointment was the following morning and I wanted to chat to Kate about all our questions for the doctor. Mostly, I wanted to know why it was so hard for everyone to find a cause for my rash; whether stem cell transplant was my only option; if I was willing to pay for immunotherapy, the side effects of which were far less aggressive, why wasn't it being offered to me? And finally, why were my biopsies so difficult to read, so unclear, on both occasions (2013 and again in 2016)?

The next morning, we caught a taxi to the hospital and made our way to the Cancer Centre. We walked through the corridors of D Block, walkways which looked so unfamiliar, but would become second nature to me in time. Upstairs were the haematology suites and downstairs was the Day Ward. We made our way to the first floor, let one of the reception staff know that I had arrived, and took a seat in the waiting room. We were preoccupied with the hope that this would be something different, that it would feel safer and my direction would feel more purposeful.

A tall, gentle-faced man wearing a bow tie came into the waiting room. He said 'Karina?' Kate and I got up, shook his hand and followed him into his office. He was very softly spoken, and I could see he was very serious about his work. We made some chit chat about Rick, he asked me to call him David and we then quickly got down to business. He told me that very little information had been sent by my haematologist and he asked to hear my story so far. I relayed what seemed to be a never-ending saga of doctors and illnesses, debilitating nausea and now this rash. I explained how there was a rash and there was an itch. The rash would come and go but the itch was with me always in varying degrees of ferocity. On this day, there was no rash, but I showed David photos of the blanketing redness that had been. I had brought with me the pathology results from the McCallum Centre and as we were discussing the report, his lab rang.

I heard him tell his colleague that I was with him. They talked in medical terms for quite a few minutes. He referred to the pathology report I had brought with me, and after some time, he hung up. He reiterated what I had heard before. It was a complex sample. David told me that his haematology lab was one of the top three in the world. That was comforting. He told me the result of the biopsy was still unclear, but it wasn't Hodgkin lymphoma. I felt like I'd been slapped in the face. Kate straight away asked if it was possible that it was not cancer after all and recounted the diagnosis of benign hamartoma in 2013. He thought deeply, then spoke. 'Look, everything's possible, but I would be surprised. We'll know more soon but the itch is typical of a type of lymphoma, but let's wait and see what the lab confirms'.

This I had not expected. Not Hodgkin. So many questions hit me. Was this why my diagnosis in 2013 had been so difficult to pin down? Was it not Hodgkin

Lymphoma even then? Is that why I had 'relapsed' so quickly, because I was given the wrong treatment? Non-Hodgkin lymphoma chemotherapy is not ABVD but goes by the acronym CHOP. Can HL change into NHL? How can one lab diagnose HL and his lab say it isn't? These questions were extremely important to get answered. They affected everything. If I was incorrectly treated the first time, it couldn't be called a relapse and then those statistics didn't apply to me. I presented David with all these questions. He agreed that they were extremely important also, but we would just have to wait.

I told David I would like him to be my doctor. We chatted about how I would manage being so far from home when sickness from treatment would inevitably strike. I told him I would have to work it out, but now with this negation of what I had been told I had, there was no way I could be treated at home. The trust I lacked had just been compounded by this further news. Not Hodgkin Lymphoma. Good God.

*

As we wandered through the corridors of this huge

hospital, Kate rang her sisters and let them know where we were at. I spoke to my brothers and all, like us, were blown away. Just as it had been for us, they were filled with anger, confusion and fear. It's enough to have cancer. But to feel that there may have been errors in treatment was heartbreaking. Who had me, indeed!

I had a chest x-ray, blood test and another PET as it had been some time since my pre-biopsy PET and David wanted to gauge the pace of the disease. When I returned to him for all these results, I learned that there had been little change from the previous PET and so we knew it wasn't fast moving. What a relief. Most importantly, the lab had come back with their final diagnosis. I had peripheral T-cell Non-Hodgkin lymphoma, two of the symptoms of which were typically rash and itching. No words. Just rage. Diagnosis of 2013 aside, in 2016 a lab had 'called' my diagnosis as Hodgkin relapse and it was not. I had complained about a rash for months and nobody raised the possibility that it could be this rare form of NHL. Again, no words. If felt like the oversights of PJP all over again. I needed time to calm and consider all the offshoots of uncertainty this diagnosis created. It would take some time to understand the true enormity of how this all would or could affect me going forward. Had I ever had Hodgkin lymphoma? I wanted my slides of 2013 to go to David's lab, which was fairly straightforward, I had hoped. It would prove an enormous task, toward which I would have to persist for over a year.

I resolved to return to Perth as soon as David felt he was ready for me to start treatment. I was to have a lung function test to make sure my damaged lungs could withstand a transplant. If all was adequate, which it proved to be, I would start treatment in a month's time. I returned home once again needing time to accept and prepare myself for a treatment I vowed I would not have due to its risks. Five per cent mortality rate of stem cell transplant, I had originally been told. Five people out of one hundred is a lot when its personal and it's not just a statistic. WA statistics were two per cent, three extra people who got to live. David gave me hope, not by his words but by taking care of how I felt when in his presence. This was humanity, easing my disorientation and helping me face what I knew would be a hard, hard road.

If I wasn't going to just allow myself to die in the grip of this disease, the only other choice I could see was to come to Western Australia and let David and his team give me a chance at life. As David had said, stem cell transplant was my best chance of survival.

The Biggest Battle Begins

The month at home was helpful. I did much of my work for my dad's business in advance with the hope that I would be home in three months. By this alone, it was obvious I really didn't understand the full implications of what I was about to undertake. I knew with the conditioning treatment to prepare me for transplant, it would be about three months. What I hadn't understood was what comes after transplant.

I made myself read about the process so I could understand it more fully. But each time I tried, I found it impossible to contain my anxiety and I could feel myself flood with panic. I saw no point in pushing myself beyond what was tolerable. A step at a time, we had said three years ago. Years on, I still felt it was how I could cope. I knew having a PICC line inserted was the first in a long list of procedures. And like during my first diagnosis, to focus on anything more was too much. I was doing okay.

After all, it wasn't too long ago that I was so immobilised by fear and mistrust that I felt my only choice was to accept my prognosis of death within a year. I was doing well. I was getting there, one step at a time.

The day before I left my home and my family my hands were so swollen and stinging with rash and itch that it was hard to dress or even drive. I felt exhausted from nights awake scratching, and the draining symptoms of lymphoma. I had gone to spend my last day with Dean, his wife, Helen and my mother. I felt safe there. There was nothing to explain and we just sat with Elisabeth and Philippa and their babies, all probably feeling the same trepidation but glad we were together. My mother had found it hard to say goodbye to me. She was saddened that she felt her age stood in the way of doing anything practical to take care of me. The reality was though, that she had given the most meaningful thing of all to help me. She was happy to fly my children and my brother Dean over, each in turn to look after me when the treatment required. There was nothing greater that I would have needed or wanted, and I felt moved that my parents' years of self-denial had enabled them to give me this gift. I felt lucky and deeply grateful.

Elisabeth stayed with me that final night and when I woke, my thighs were covered with a carpet of red, hot and angry rash. I messaged David and asked him whether I could take some dexamethasone; coupled with the condition of my hands, it felt overwhelming. He asked me not to take anything and wait for the biopsy. I boarded my flight later that day, with my legs and hands pulsing with heat and an unrelenting sting. It was a hard five hours.

I arrived at my hotel and explained to the front desk that I really didn't know how long I would be staying and whether most of my time would be spent in hospital or in my hotel room. They asked me to let them know if there was anything they could do to help me. It touched me. They could see I was alone, and they offered me kindness that helped me feel as safe as one can feel in a strange city, in a strange hotel, waiting for a strange procedure.

That night, as was the routine, I woke with the usual stinging and hot inflamed rash. I drew a cold bath. I sat in what felt like freezing cold water in contrast to the heat of my legs, feet and hands. In the middle of this night, I had some lonely realizations. As I sat there with my teeth chattering, I thought about where I was, why I was there, and feeling how uncertain the future was. I had been dancing with death for so long – since 2009. Now it was almost 2017. It was a lot. I was exhausted and a feeling of deep loneliness, of hopelessness, came over me.

I sat and waited for relief to come. Until it did, I just noticed how deeply sad I felt. I eventually got out of the bath, gently patted myself dry trying not to stimulate too much blood flow to my rash and lay in bed as still as I could. Thankfully I drifted off to sleep. When I woke, I thought immediately of my girls. Elisabeth, Philippa and their babies were arriving in a couple of days to be with me during the start of treatment. I was excited to see them. I knew we all had work to do, but that aside, just being close to each other brought such comfort. My job was to present my body to those who knew how to give it the best chance of healing. My girls and Dean had under-taken the task of keeping me safe and well when I couldn't look after myself. I knew from experience that once the toxic drugs accumulated in my system, I would become almost helpless. I also knew it would cost my children and my brother Dean a lot in terms of coordinating their lives. It was a mammoth impost on them and like before, it was hard to receive without guilt.

Despite this guilt, one of the greatest lessons I had already learned is that until it happens, it is impossible to understand what real helplessness is and how totally a person must rely on family and friends when it hits. It is both humbling and chastening, and once experienced, can never be forgotten. What also came with it for me was a lesson in gratitude. Gratitude for those who loved me and were willing to give so wholeheartedly. My dear friend Michael once shared with me a simultaneously comforting and challenging idea that I've never forgotten. 'Once you know, you can't un-know,' he said. So now I know, I can't un-know the depth of goodness that surrounds me. I try each day not to let pettiness and superficial hurts interfere with my gratitude for others' selflessness.

*

It was late October when I attended D Block once again. I had come to discuss with David what I needed to do next. He was concerned about my accommodation in a hotel. Unlike me, he knew the months ahead could be more like six than three. How would it work, especially when I became frail and unable to look after myself? I let David know that we felt that the only choice for treatment was in WA with him and we were just going to have to make it work. Now of course, I understand totally why he was so concerned: our belief that we were ready for what would come was unrealistic and lacking real understanding of the process. But at the time we felt this was the only path available and we would just have to do the best we could. Rick's family all worked and the expectation of them being there to nurse me was unfair. They helped as much as they could but it would fall mostly at the feet of the hospital staff and my three girls and Dean.

I discussed with David once again, my huge challenges with nausea and how we had finally found a regime that worked during my previous nine months of chemo. He was happy to offer any drugs that I had found helped. He felt in time that Palliative Care may be able to trial some other drugs but for now he didn't want to add to my anxiety by changing the drugs I trusted. I thanked him.

I then met with the dermatology team, who biopsied the rash on my thighs. The local anaesthetic hurt more than usual. They took their samples, I had a couple of stitches and left. Cutting and bodily intrusions had become familiar and my pain tolerance over the years had increased dramatically. It was never pleasant, but I had learned that the discomfort eventually passes.

I returned to the hotel to wait for the arrival of Elisabeth, Philippa and the babies. Whilst I did, I finally was able to gulp down some dexamethasone and by evening, when they arrived, I was experiencing some relief from the sting and heat. My mother had arranged for the girls to be on the same floor as me, with cots ready for the babies. It was great to see them, and we spent that evening chatting and trying to relax. With one baby at one year and the other at five months, it was a real challenge for them, especially as the youngest was still being breastfed. In the days ahead, they would take turns babysitting both babies; while one stayed the other would come with me to the hospital. It was difficult. They swore to me it was no trouble and they were exactly where they wanted to be, but I understood how hard it was and I felt moved by how they managed it together.

*

Tests completed, it was now time to begin treatment. It had been a long road to get to this point, and on this day, I felt both disquiet and readiness. Philippa and I returned to the hospital and I was directed to a bed in Day Ward where I waited to be taken to have my PICC inserted. I didn't really understand what this entailed except I knew there was a ten per cent chance of PICC lines becoming infected. I swore to myself to be hypervigilant with sanitizing my hands constantly. After an hour or so of waiting, I was wheeled away, leaving Philippa behind. The line was inserted by two lovely women who chatted with me about their lives and mine. They fed the tube with a wire inside to guide it, up my armpit and across my chest, lining up with my heart. It was not painless but certainly not traumatic, considering a wire was just fed through my body. When in position, the wire was removed, leaving the tube in place. At the entry point, there were two lumens into which drugs and fluids could be administered. It took about half an hour after which I was x-rayed to see if the line was placed correctly. As I was wheeled from the x-ray room, Philippa had come and found me. Her smiling face at seeing me relaxed and okay was wonderful. The first step was over.

I was wheeled back into the Day Ward to be told that chemo could not start that day as there were no beds on the haematology ward. I would have to return home and ring the next day to see if there was a bed free. Whilst this was frustrating, I actually felt I had done enough for one day. There was discomfort across my chest which I later found out was a muscle spasm in response to the PICC being inserted. Not dangerous, but uncomfortable, so I was happy to go back to the hotel with Philippa and rest.

We spent the afternoon calling room service and playing with the babies. Even though the discomfort across my chest was bothersome, the afternoon was lovely. Mindfulness had been such a useful lesson I had learned many years ago. Being in the moment. And in those moments, I had four human beings I loved deeply with me as we ate club sandwiches and played and laughed. It was nice to notice how amidst it all, there were such lovely times.

*

It took another three days until a bed became available, and even though the girls had come for a different reason, spending time together and forgetting about chemo and hospitals for those days in between was a welcome surprise. When I got the okay to come in, we all felt quietly sad that reality had struck again but at the same time, we knew that it was time to get on with it. It was afternoon when Philippa and I arrived at the hospital. The room we were shown to was clean and sunny. They kept the ward very cold, I'm not sure why. A lovely nurse asked me to put on a gown to make the infusion easier and I popped into my bed. We waited for the bags of chemicals to arrive and as we did, there was a strong feeling of having been here before. Not geographically of course, but emotionally and spiritually. What was different for us all was that we had placed our trust in this man, to get me to the other side. I knew he could feel the weight of my reliance on that fact. Maybe unfair. Probably. But without that belief, I would still be lying in my bed at home, trying to adjust to the fact that I was going to die within the year. Even as I write these words, I am finding it hard to breathe from panic at remembering how that felt. I hope he understood that his warmth and connection gave me the courage to try. I knew the rest was in God's hands.

Philippa had to return home to the babies and I waited with these thoughts circling my head. While I drifted off, a nurse (who I would get to know well) walked in gowned up and pushing a trolley with bags filled with clear liquid. I heard myself agreeing to all her questions, knowing whilst my mouth was saying yes, my heart was saying no. No, I don't understand why I was having this treatment. No, I don't agree to it and no, I don't accept that there would be some dangerous side effects that I must look for. But I knew the outcome if I uttered those 'nos'. There was no way out. I tried to relax and just let it happen.

I spent the next few days in hospital receiving the first round of a regime they called HI-DICE. My body still had not overtly registered the presence of these chemicals within it, so the potency of the assault was not yet evident. I felt hopeful. However, I knew the path, and feared what more than likely would come. As the time to leave hospital came, I did not return to the hotel. There was to be a three-week break from the first infusion until the next and Rick and his family had also become concerned about my plans to return to the hotel. It was not their job to be a part of this path I'd chosen so far from home, but I was grateful when they invited me to stay with them. I knew they all worked and had no spare rooms, so I had never considered this as an option. Wanting to minimise the impact on others was always in my mind. To make room for me, my nephew, Oliver (in his twenties) had given up his room and offered to sleep on a mattress on the floor of his father's study. Considering the length of time I would need it, it was a huge gesture and as always, I was grateful.

The expected happened in the middle of the first week after infusion. I became more and more nauseated. I tried to walk it off, take everything, including my faithful Phenergan, but it was beating me. Elisabeth sat by my bed with my niece trying to help in whatever way they could, but it was quite hopeless. I was left no choice other than to attend ED feeling acutely motion sick. All drug attempts failed or merely dampened the feeling. It felt like I was holding my head in my hands, eyes closed, for days on end, praying for it to stop.

Ultimately, I was admitted to the ward and rehydrated. This helped me feel a little more present, but did little to help any nausea. Amidst all the attempts by nursing staff to alleviate the discomfort, there was a knock on the door by the head of the Palliative Care Team. His name was Dominic. I cried when he introduced himself. I really didn't understand what a blessing he was until we started to chat. I explained that nausea would come slowly and then if not caught by some remedial drug, would gain such strength that nothing seemed to work. He asked me what I had used in the past. I told him. He listened kindly and totally. His head shook when he heard I had spent ten out of fourteen days incapacitated by nausea in my last nine-month treatment. He assured me there were many other drugs we could try that would give me the ability to endure treatment much more comfortably. I cried again. It was becoming a pattern. He suggested I see the counsellor on the ward. I agreed. But first he would begin trying drugs that he hoped would give me some relief.

I didn't have to wait long. A drug called cyclizine was injected into my PICC. It was pushed in slowly due to its strength and almost immediately I felt relief flood my body. What had been such obstinate nausea for years now, was so easily quietened by the first drug Dominic had suggested. I didn't know how to thank him. He explained to me that the way to manage nausea was the same as managing pain. Keep it under control so it doesn't gain the momentum that necessitates large doses of drugs to pull it back. I was to have this drug prophylactically via IV throughout my admissions and hopefully I would be able to manage on oral cyclizine when home. It felt like a miracle, allowing me to sidestep this unforgiving side effect of treatment. After my initial cyclizine injection, a modicum of hope was restored within me that I may be able to endure treatment if I was to be ushered through with this same sort of care each time a health challenge arose. I prayed it would be so.

Naming It

One of the concepts I know so well in my work as a therapist is that naming the truth of what goes on inside each of us is the first step toward emotional healing. So hard is it for some, including myself, to admit that anger, jealousy, hatred, or any other shameful feeling resides within them, that they create stories around their feelings that justify them. I remember learning to recognise this in myself. I still feel shame at each of these feelings when I have them, but now I know that denial doesn't diminish them. And finding justifications for them only complicates an admission that may be painful but quite uncomplicated, when we have the courage to face it.

What I needed to name was that I was in deep grief. I knew it. In some ways I understood why –I was facing an illness that can kill. But it was deeper. It was about a lack of safety and control. A lack of trust. It was grief mixed with terror and my eye was too close to the penny to understand what was going on. What I did know was that I cried often, I felt terrified all the time and I was convinced that I was going to die. I had never really recovered faith in life since PJP and after my second lymphoma diagnosis I was plunged into this type of grief so deeply that I was unable to climb out. Only once before had I felt grief like this. It was when my father died. But it lacked the terror then, a terror that now coupled with the mortifying grief. I needed help, there was no doubt.

*

Jeremy knocked on my door one morning as I lay in my hospital bed. 'Got time to chat?' he said as he poked his head in. 'Sure,' I answered. He let me know he was the ward therapist and it had been suggested that perhaps I needed to talk about some things. Immediately my eyes welled up and I nodded my head. It was hard to share. Being a therapist myself, I felt ashamed I couldn't figure it out. I know now that healing a broken heart with a broken heart was a lot to ask of myself.

Jeremy was kind and listened with the intensity that I

would have hoped for. Just like both David and Dominic before him. I could see that the ideal of compassion trickled down from the top of this haematology team.

We talked about my shock the day of re-diagnosis. About how I could only explain it the way I had done so previously, on so many other occasions. That my heart broke. I had always imagined this was a metaphor. But I now believed it to be an actual state of being. My chest ached, I could actually feel the disruption to my heart's function. It hurt. I had been in agony, a feeling that had persisted up until the moment of his arrival. This agony was coupled with lost hope and initially, immobility to do anything to save myself. There was a resignation to death whilst at the same time terror that would wake me in the night breathless. He listened carefully, asking questions when he needed to, but otherwise just listening. We talked about the shame I felt. All the stories of heroism so often depicted in the news and books about cancer patients. I was not one of these. I told myself I was a coward because I wanted to run as far away from myself and my life's path as my feet could possibly take me. But I knew that wherever I ran, my cancer would come too. Writing now I feel the depletion of energy I had always felt at that time and to some extent still do. No energy to do what was necessary. I had put one foot in front of the other to get here. It had been a journey like going up a down escalator in its pace and energy required. Only I was walking it with terror and grief.

It was time for Jeremy to go. I felt like my guts had spilled over the floor in the hour we had spent together. It wasn't easy to admit all these feelings and I felt vulnerable. He was reassuring and said he would come twice a week, so we could chat about these and any other issues that arose for me. It felt both a relief and excruciating to own up to my lack of courage, and I hoped that sharing it may ease its sting.

After Jeremy left, I reflected on how once again I was moved by another member of David's team. For me, this ethos that was apparent in those I had met so far was a game changer. It evoked a feeling of being held at last. I was being watched, the team alerted of anything threatening. Crucially, there was a human connection that didn't overlook the person travelling under their care. My current hope for this kind of spirit in medicine, but especially when dealing with terminal illnesses, was born from walking amongst this team and experiencing what they did differently. Their understanding of humanity, just so important, gave me a sense of dignity and self-determination throughout my treatment.

Most importantly and memorably, I would come to rely on their gentleness and kindness at the times I was closest to death, usually from resilient infections coupled with my juvenile – and defenseless – bone marrow.

These difficult times were all to come. On this day, after my first visit from Jeremy, I was not yet aware the role all the team would play in managing each knock my body and my spirit encountered. That day, I just knew I had named it. And it was a relief.

Hard Truths

It was now only a matter of days before I had to return for my second treatment. I felt weak, but nausea was manageable on oral cyclizine, so I was able to go home. I could move around and interact with the family and it felt like it had been ten months not ten days since I had last been home. My three girls had been back and forward through this time and Dean would come in a few days for my next round. In the meantime, my sister-in-law Bron tried to get me out and away from medicine and we decided to go for a coffee and maybe a bite if I could manage it. I hadn't realised that leaving a chair was so exhausting, but it was lovely to be in the fresh air and amongst people doing their daily chores and just enjoying life. How jealous I felt of 'normal.' Would I ever know 'normal' again?

We sat in a small Italian restaurant and I could feel myself shake with weakness. I knew I was quiet and not much company, but I did my best to take part in regular life. As my nephew, niece, Bron and I sat there, I noticed strands of my hair slowly floating onto the white tablecloth. The time for this had come. The beginning of the transformation, once again. I made an instant decision to have my head shaved after lunch. This was part of what was expected, and it held no meaning anymore. Yes, it was visible evidence of cancer, but this time around, it mattered little as my problem was no longer shock at thinking of myself as a cancer patient. I had not felt like anything else for many years now. My challenge in these days was accepting that I may never again feel like anything but a cancer patient. I knew once I entered hospital, hair loss would only increase in volume, so there was no sense in delaying the inevitable. Yes, after lunch, I would have it taken care of.

Although quite woozy, it was nice to listen to my family chat during lunch, to look out into the sunshine and to eat a little pasta, which I hoped would give me some energy. All my life I had worried about what I weighed, expecting to weigh in my fifties what I weighed in my twenties. Interestingly, it had never been underpinned by any virtuous reason, but purely to look my best. My focus was no longer on my exterior. I wanted to nurture my interior in the hope it would forgive me for any part I had played in its breakdown. No more soft drinks with chemical sweeteners, no fast food, no junk food. The horse may have bolted, but it was all I had in my power to do: to respect my failing body.

We eventually left the restaurant and walked a short distance to the hairdresser. I could see the hairdresser was saddened by what I was asking. I felt for her. Cancer is confronting for everyone. As she shaved my head, she was quiet. When finished, she asked if it was okay. 'Yes, thank you,' I replied. We walked to the register and she said that it was free of charge. 'No, no,' I protested. She insisted. Just as with my previous haircut from Dan, I was deeply moved.

We went home to rest and I donned my cap to keep my head warm. I sent a photo to my girls and family and they all told me how beautiful I looked. They made me smile. I always felt so loved; their care was not lost on me. It always felt lucky. God's blessings always stood out for me.

*

Dean arrived after a few days and together we went to stay at the hotel for the two nights before my admission. I had been notified by the hospital that I had an appointment to meet with the Cancer Outreach Nurse, Vicky, to hear about the upcoming process. I asked Dean if he would come with me. I was not really sure what we had to discuss as I knew that the next round was to be the same as the first and now with cyclizine, it held less anxiety for me. But I was told it was an important discussion, so we attended the waiting room and waited our turn.

I introduced Dean to Vicky, and after some friendly banter, we sat down with her to go through some papers she had in front of her. Pretty soon, I understood that the information I was about to hear was that which I had avoided up until now. The detail of what was to be done to me. As much as I didn't want to know, I had no choice now as I needed to sign off on risks and understand danger signs. It felt dark.

Dean sat beside me and together we heard the following. I would have my next round of chemotherapy and remain in hospital where nausea and side effects would be kept under control. Straight after treatment, I would be given injections daily in my stomach, to promote the manufacture of new stem cells. These injections may create back pain and I was to ask for pain relief should this occur. Some people need morphine others only Panadol. Each day blood tests would determine whether there seemed to be enough stem cells for harvest. Once this number was reached, I was to have a Vascath inserted into my neck. It was a tube that had the thickness of a biro and had long tendrils coming off it. From this the stem cell harvest was made. I would be attached to a machine that would take from my neck the blood containing the stem cells, sift them out, and return the remaining blood to me. It sounded space age. I may need to repeat this for a few days to gather enough and then the Vascath would be removed from my neck and the stem cells frozen. I wondered how I would sleep with this occupant in my neck. Although this was matter of least importance in the grand scheme of things, I realised.

Then I would have a PET. This was to see if the disease had been killed by the two rounds of chemo. If not, I would have to have a third and if not again, we would have to meet and discuss what to do next. The thought of it not working sent my heart pounding, panic starting to rise.

She went on. If the results showed the disease had been killed, I would have my PICC line removed. I would take a three-week break for Christmas and return on the 27th December for the transplant stage of treatment. I would have my PICC replaced by a central line in my neck. Through this line, five separate days of very strong chemo would be administered to kill my bone marrow, some days receiving eight hours of chemo in a row. The final day involved a drug that would require me to suck on ice constantly for three hours. This was to avoid mouth ulcers. This same drug would cause intense diarrhea. I would also be very susceptible to infections for quite some time, with my bone marrow having been killed off.

Finally, I would have a day's rest and then have the harvested stem cells transplanted back over the course of an hour or so. From this time onward, there would be a large risk of illness; this is the critical stage of treatment. Some people are able to go home and come back each time they suffer an infection, but due to my fragility in the past, and my lung issues, I would be remaining in hospital.

Dean asked some questions, but I was so afraid that I

could barely absorb what was being said. This wasn't a step at a time. This was a huge leap and it was too much even though I knew it had to be talked about. I had gone into shock and as Dean and I left we were speechless. We sat on a bench nearby. We both had tears in our eyes, sitting in a very scary emotional place, anticipating a process so dangerous and so invasive. We rang Rick. My panic was hard to contain, and we asked him if he could provide some Valium for me, so I could sleep. Of course, he said.

*

That evening the breathlessness of panic would come and go. I encouraged Dean to have dinner with the family as I was in no state to be of any company. I needed to take my Valium and try and watch some TV to take my mind somewhere else. Earlier that day, I checked with the hospital whether there was a bed available for me. At that time, there was not. In some way I was relieved as I had a lot to process before I returned for treatment 2.

I rested that night with chemical help, and in the morning, I dressed and met Dean for a semblance of

156

breakfast. The comfort I felt having him sit with me in my silence was without measure. No advice, no platitudes, just love in the form of being there quietly, trying to eat together and, importantly, remain calm. After breakfast he encouraged me to take a walk in the fresh air with him. As we did, we started talking about our life as children, our misunderstandings in our adulthood and the things we had learned about life at these our more mature years. It was so easy to talk about things that had once seemed so important to defend. None of it mattered but the closeness our conversation brought about was a magical gift. My life with him would never be the same. We were sharing something that, fortunately, most will never experience, but as before, God's blessings always stood out. My future was sketchy, and I ached to live to be with my children and grandchildren. But on that day I recognised a gift: I got to know my brother in a way that only the threat of death could have evoked. Inside my head, I said thank you.

*

We spent the day this way, stopping to rest, eat and at

other times just sit quietly. At two o'clock, I received a phone call from the hospital and was told a bed had become available. It was time to be brave. I prayed I could find it within me. I packed my bag and checked out of the hotel and Dean and I made our way to the hospital.

As I unpacked my toiletries and clothes, David's registrar Sanjay arrived. Once again, this young man was a human being before a doctor. He had compassion and heart and exhibited it by giving time and understanding to me (and I'm sure all his patients on the ward). He asked me if I was ready and I said 'no' as I laughed. I hopped into bed and as Dean and I waited for the chemo to arrive, I started to feel nausea hit me strong and hard. It was powerful, and debilitating and I was confused as to why I felt so ill when I had not received any treatment yet.

Sanjay returned and sat on my bedside as I held my head in my hands. 'I'm so sorry,' I said, 'I don't know what's happening.' He sat quietly and held my hand. He reassured me that I wasn't letting anyone down, explaining that this response was quite normal especially when nausea had been such a challenge for me. He explained that some patients who have had bad nausea from chemo often get anticipatory nausea, which is no less real. The body anticipates what will be happening and responds with what normally happens. He told me we had all day and to just take it easy. I felt so ashamed and told him so, but he repeated that I wasn't letting anyone down and just to try and relax. He would give me some cyclizine, which should alleviate the nausea. Then they could get on with the infusion as soon as I felt ready.

Dean sat quietly in the background. I apologised to him that I wasn't braver. Even if my head told me I could manage, my body had found it too much. How helpless and embarrassed I felt. He told me how brave he thought I was. I couldn't understand how he felt this way when I felt so ashamed. The nurse came in with cyclizine, and as she pushed it slowly into my PICC, I felt relief from both the panic and the nausea. I lay back into my pillow and the tears of relief filled my eyes.

*

By the time the chemo arrived, it was late afternoon, nearly dinner. I told Dean once again to go and eat with the family. It had been a big day for both of us and he needed to go and rest and recharge. I would be fine. I knew what to expect for this step and whilst my nausea was under control, I felt fine just to sit back and be with my thoughts. My niece, Olivia came and collected him, her smiling face always putting one on mine. I was glad he'd be away from the hospital for a time. This part was new to him, and I knew he would find it as hard as I did the first time to watch toxic medicines enter my body, trying to make sense of it all. At some point I fell asleep, only to be woken for cyclizine. With its four-hourly help, I rested well and before I knew it, I saw Dean's face pop in. It was morning and I smiled when I saw him. Cyclizine not only contained my nausea but made me sleepy and sedate. It was to be the last day of Dean's visit and while the second day's chemo was administered he read his book beside me as I dozed.

At some point that morning Sanjay popped his head in to see how I was going. Also, Dominic from Pall Care. David Joske came with his team. And finally, Jeremy. I was so pleased that Dean got to meet these people, who were so major in making this experience radically differ-ent from my first. He was moved by them all and when Jeremy sat down for our session, I asked Dean if he would like to stay. Jeremy asked him how he was coping with seeing his sister go through this experience. He was so surprised to have been asked. I've always believed that cancer reaches everyone that cares about the cancer sufferer. Each has their battles, and each is entitled to feel however they feel. David's team understood this, and Dean had an opportunity to share some of his feelings. I felt privileged to witness his honesty.

Later that afternoon it was time for Dean to fly home. My girls would arrive in a week and I told him I would be fine. Rick and his family were there, and they would visit me constantly. We hugged and said our goodbyes. I let him know how much him coming had meant to me and he left to catch his flight.

Harvest

I felt weak and pale after the second round of treatment. The drugs were beginning to compound in my body, wearing me down. I had no appetite for anything other than salad, which was not permitted in hospital due to my low neutrophil count. But the more affected I felt by the drugs, the more deeply placated I was by the hope that this round was doing its job.

One evening around midnight I lay waiting for my dose so I could go to sleep undisturbed for four hours, when the silence on the ward was broken by the cries of a patient calling out in pain. Him begging, 'Please, please!' and 'I can't, I can't,' filled me with fear, both for him and me. His suffering reminded me of the down-on-the-ground cruelty of this disease, and how hard it was to remove myself from the ever-present reality of those who had exhausted their avenues of hope, who were just being treated for the consequences as their cancers took over. Was this to be my future too? Pain so severe that it drove a person to beg? I heard the nurses scurry and call back to him that they would be there very soon; they were just drawing up his pain relief. As he moaned into his pillow I felt so helpless and frightened. Soon I heard them say, 'Here we go,' and in minutes he had become quiet and presumably fell asleep relieved by the drugs. This wasn't a lone incident. Nights on the ward were peppered with pleas like this. And it was nights like these that provided brutal evidence of the parallel world of cancer treatment, going on simultaneously to the world of those not afflicted.

When I woke the next morning, the memory of the night before saddened me. Not just for me but for all on that ward who lay there, hoping for something different. Eight years on from my first diagnosis, I wondered whether it was possible to ever kill this demon. I knew what I hoped for and what I prayed to God for, but I also wondered, just like many times before, why should I be protected from what this poor man suffered? Why was I any better or more important than him? I still couldn't find any answers to these questions, and like always, felt ashamed about asking for what others had been denied.

A nurse came in with my morning dose and I gratefully drifted off to sleep again. When I woke, Elisabeth had arrived. She was sitting quietly beside me, waiting for me to wake. I hugged and kissed her and when she asked me how my night was, I told her it had been okay. There was no point in adding salt to her wounds. She offered to take me through the grounds in a wheelchair to get away from the ward for a while.

It made me remember my father in his last weeks, and me thinking the same – that he might like to get out into the fresh air. Dean and I stubbornly ignored his desire not to, thinking it would 'do him good.' I now wanted to hold him and tell him how sorry I was for what we clumsily put him through, thinking we knew better. The very thing that I found so hard about others now, I myself had once done. Failing to listen and give respect. It was an arrogant trap and hard to own up to.

Unlike my poor father, I found the outing a nice distraction and I could see Elisabeth's loving eyes, checking to see if I was enjoying the fresh air. I trembled in the wheelchair. Even sitting up at times seemed too much. But the cool air felt nice against my skin and the colours in some of the flowers we saw were beautiful. We went into the courtyard to give Elisabeth a rest. We looked around at others looking very much like I did. Bald, yellow-skinned and struggling to sit up. Others, connected to their drips, sat having cigarettes. It always surprised me to see cancer patients in the courtyard smoking. It's not that I didn't understand the draw of smoking, as I too had once smoked in my twenties. What surprised me was that we were all fighting a disease known to develop another version of itself due to smoking. It felt strange to not be scared witless by the chance of facing this disease in another form as well as the one we now faced. It seemed like tempting the devil.

Elisabeth wheeled me back to my room where we were greeted by a nurse from Day Ward. She had come to measure my neck for the Vascath. Since the end of my second treatment, injections to my stomach had been given daily, and today's results had shown that the number of stem cells present were enough for harvest.

Ward staff left me little time to ruminate on how this might feel or to get too anxious before I left Elisabeth and was wheeled down to recovery, where an anaesthetist set up a bay for the insertion into my neck. He talked me through the whole process step by step and apologised for any discomfort I may feel. He was extremely kind and deeply humane in his understanding of what he was about to do to another human being, however necessary. It was probably the most invasive insertion so far, with the catheter being about half a centimeter in width and quite stiff. The tendrils coming off it splayed out of my neck, thick and quite cumbersome. It was hard to ignore, probably mostly because of the stiffness of the length of catheter within the vein in my neck. It took about an hour to position. It wasn't a pleasant experience, but it was doable and I felt I was doing well with each step I took toward transplant. I felt proud of myself. I was getting there slowly. It occurred to me that this experience of transplant had two arms. The first involved me completing each step of treatment. At this, I felt I had been successful. However, I had no control over the other arm. That is, ensuring that any of these efforts would result in sustained remission. This would be unknown and remain unknown for years to come. All I could focus on, if I was to get anywhere, was the part I could control. I had to just keep turning up and doing what was expected of me with the help and support of the team and the love of my family. For the rest I could only pray and trust. My next job was harvest.

*

The machines that harvested the stem cells looked similar to the crude makeshift stills to make alcohol. It wasn't apparent by looking at them that they performed such a sophisticated procedure as separating stem cells from blood. I felt quite comfortable, having just had my dose of cyclizine. So I lay back with my bed still in a zigzag to alleviate back pain, and the nurse explained what she would be doing throughout the hours I was there. Elisabeth arrived, and we chatted quietly while the nurse connected the tendrils to the machine. We were told that a side effect of this this process was that it took calcium from the blood, causing tingling in my lips. She said I could fix this by sipping on milk.

The nurse turned the machine on and as it was behind me, I could only hear it but not see it working. It sounded a little like a washing machine, unthreatening in its rhythm. As promised, slowly my lips began tingling and Elisabeth went and bought me some milk to sip on. Although this was a lengthy process, it was one of the most comfortable so far, with the worst sensations being tingly lips and accommodating what felt like a large stick in my neck. It gave Elisabeth and me, and later in the afternoon Philippa and me, an uninterrupted space to catch up on the children and their lives back home.

Hours later, I had slept and awoke to the harvest being complete. I was told they had gathered enough stem cells for two transplants and I was proud of my poor battered body for doing so well. I was wheeled back to the ward and told I could be discharged the next day and return in a week for my PET. I tried not to think about the PET for now, focusing on leaving the hospital and spending time with the girls and children.

*

The following day I felt stronger than usual, though maybe it was just the adrenalin from excitement at being discharged. Mid-morning my nurse came with a bag of platelets and told me that my platelet count was quite low, which meant she would hang a bag to avoid excessive bleeding from the large hole left by removal of the Vascath. Once I had received these platelets, she returned equipped with dressings, and after applying heavy pressure to my neck, the Vascath was removed. She applied such forceful pressure for about ten minutes that it was quite uncomfortable, but I understood why. She then applied a pressure bandage to my neck and I was free to leave with Philippa, who had come to collect me.

Elisabeth and Philippa had rented a short-stay apartment for themselves in the heart of the city, and one for me, so I could stay with them before they had to return home in three or four days. The trip from hospital had been challenging, so when I arrived at the apartment, I went straight to bed to rest. As it turned out, over the next few days, I slept a lot, battled more frequently with nausea, but managed to keep it under control with oral drugs. I was finally able to eat freshly made salad my children prepared; this was all that felt doable. I craved it at every mealtime and the girls made sure there was plenty. Food in hospitals is not good at the best of times, but when one is immune-suppressed, the selection becomes even more wanting. It was so quiet away from the bustle of a hospital, and having the girls looking after my nutrition and water intake allowed me to just lie back and heal from the last round.

After the first full day of just sleeping, the greatest joy was seeing my grandchildren, whom I hadn't seen for over two months. My grandson Jack, who was old enough to have had a relationship with me before I left, noticed that my hair had gone. I could see him staring at my head and when he crawled over to me, Elisabeth sat him in my lap and he began taking my hat off and on, checking out what had happened that was different. I had been so worried my baldness and sallowness would scare him. But to my surprise, he found removing and replacing my hat funny, a game. He looked at the pressure bandage on my neck and then at my face. I smiled at him as he looked uncertain, and this seemed to be enough to make him feel all was well.

I had tried hard to maintain contact with Jack via iPhone videos whilst I was in hospital. Each day, I would video myself saying good morning to him and I would sing him one of his favourite songs like I did when we had been together. Elisabeth would video him watching my video with her iPad. He always said 'Yiayia!' and bounced to the songs he knew so well. Elisabeth said he watched them over and over and would kiss the screen. It was such a joy for me and I too would watch the videos of him over and over.

For Chloe it was harder. She was only a couple of months old when I received my diagnosis and we had missed those important weeks of me holding her and her getting to know my scent and face. She was unsure of me and cried most times I held her. Whilst this was sad, I knew if all went well, I would have time for her to slowly become familiar with me. I understood that to her I was a stranger, particularly now looking so different to anything she may have remembered. I would love her from a distance until our time to get to know each other came.

One of the losses I feared, and one that urged me to find the courage for transplant, was that of my grandchildren not knowing their mother's mother. And I wanted to watch them grow and feel loved by me. To share this incredible experience with my children would be the very biggest gift.

*

A few days later, the girls returned home and I removed the pressure bandage from my neck. Apart from twice-weekly visits to the hospital to have blood tests and a lung function test, I was able to take a break until my PET. It became a lovely time, being home with the Perth family as they prepared for Christmas and shows on TV started to have happy Christmas specials on. We went out a few times and whilst it was exhausting, it was also a glimpse of normal.

But after some days, I had noticed my lungs starting to be challenged and after a night of shallow breathing whilst asleep, I found it hard for them to draw enough air when I got up. It felt all too familiar. I started using a nebuliser, which made it a little freer to breathe. However, getting out and about was becoming a harsher story as each day went by.

The day of my PET arrived, and my girls or Dean had not yet returned. The family in Perth were all at work, so I attended on my own. It was a trial getting there via taxi as the short walk to and from the car left me gasping. I moved incrementally, by sitting at every opportunity and giving myself short distance goals to the next chair. I arrived at last at Nuclear Medicine and went through the procedure I knew so well. So challenged was I by walking and being able to get air, that it gave me little time to panic over the PET and its results. Second time around was definitely a tougher proposition than treatment in 2013 and of course it made perfect sense. My body had already been through the fire once. It had never really recovered. What I did know was that I wasn't a well person either way.

I felt like I was suffocating as I walked back into the house. I dropped onto the couch and tried to find a posture which made it easier to breathe, heaving as I did. After about twenty minutes I started to recover. Once again, just like with PJP, I feared such straining would be too much for my heart. I was getting to understand the dangers of transplant on a chemo-wearied body, and I hadn't even had the bone-marrow-killing chemo yet. I started to doubt whether I would be able to withstand the journey. As my breath came back and I could think more clearly, I decided to let David know that I didn't think my lungs were holding up to treatment.

*

Each day seemed a little harder even though I was using a nebuliser now several times a day. I messaged Vicky and she told me to come in. She paged David and he arrived to witness what was happening. He looked worried and sent me for a chest x-ray. Walking there was again a chair to chair proposition and I kicked myself for not asking for a wheelchair. I returned to Vicky once x-rayed; by now, I needed to lie down and my head was thumping from lack of air. I was so afraid of what my body was going through so early in treatment.

Once I recovered adequately enough to chat to David, he said my chest x-rays showed what he thought was an infection. However, due to my history of PJP, rather than commence me on broad spectrum antibiotics, he decided to start me on large doses of Bactrim. By that evening, I was vomiting at every dose. I tried crushing the tablets or cutting them up, but I continued to vomit them up. When I messaged Vicky, she told me to stop and return to the hospital the next day. Thankfully, Bron was able to drop me and when I arrived, I was given a medicated nebuliser and kept away from all other patients who were also immune suppressed. I was given different antibiotics, which I seemed to tolerate better. Coupled with ampoules of the nebuliser meds, this made life momentarily doable.

What had I been thinking when I decided I could stay

in a hotel and look after myself in between family visits? I couldn't even manage to get in and out of taxis without a struggle. But this is what I had chosen, in order to have a doctor I felt safe with. This is how it had to be and whatever difficulties I faced were borne out of that decision. I had to remember that.

Merry Christmas?

My mind was on my PET. I knew this determined the type of Christmas all of us would have. I tried to adjust to the idea that I may need a third round of chemo, and as affected as my lungs had become by the first two treatments, I was more worried about what it may mean for me if the third did not provide me with a clear PET. It was a constant battle, trying to keep morale up. A constant internal dialogue of 'Why me?' against, 'Why not me?' when praying for a clear PET.

I was constantly brought back to the emotional struggle that facing death brings. A dangling carrot of *maybe survival*, toggling against a *maybe not*.

I made a huge mistake sharing this struggle with my children. They wanted to see me overcoming all in the quest for success. I could see their eyes weary. I shared with Jeremy that sometimes I felt angry that anybody wanted anything from me. But then I'd remember, I'm a mother of amazingly committed children and where on earth was my gratitude? It was a difficult place to sit. I wanted to make everything easier for my girls, but sometimes out of a weakened body, I was less than enough for them.

For this reason, the lead up to Christmas was difficult for us all. All the girls, who were now in their thirties, had decided to come with their families to spend Christmas with me; Elisabeth and Philippa would stay with me for transplant in January. We all stayed in an apartment complex and I tried my best to cover up how I was feeling. I would wait for nighttime so I could just let go and be. What made it worse was that when I visited David to learn that my PET results were good, I didn't feel any less morose. I had cried with relief when David told me, and my children were understandably elated. But they couldn't understand why for me, nothing had changed. I, to this day, do not understand why I still felt so afraid. I think this was probably the most difficult time for the girls, especially for Kate, who shared an apartment with me. 'Tell me what's wrong,' she would say. In those moments I didn't feel like anyone's mother. I couldn't spare her and pretend. I wished so deeply that I could.

But my heart was wholly broken and I wondered if I would ever feel safe, no matter what happened.

I mention these feelings to reach those who may have felt the same, to enable them to feel less lonely. To not feel unlovable as I at times did. How I felt is how I felt. I exhibited no heroics, just the 'on your knees' kind of behaviour this illness can evoke when it dominates life for eight years. I had always sensed that something broke inside me on that day of relapse diagnosis and I feared it was irreparable. It was an incredibly lonely place.

*

Outside this emotional turmoil, Christmas Day was such a wonderful day. Bron had cooked an amazing meal for my whole family and hers. I loved her more than ever that day. She gave my family something I could not. And she gave it with such love and warmth. I simply watched everyone enjoying themselves, my Perth family laughing and caring for my Sydney family. It was such a welcome break from confusion and fear. I tried to stay in the moment and relish these expressions of love. I will never forget them.

The last eight years had seen many examples of such deep love, I had thought to myself as I sat quietly and watched the day pass. I thought of friends who held me with personal knowledge of these kinds of treatments. Many had lost parents to this ugliness and understood what it did. Two dear friends would message me with snapshots of life back home, funny incidences, photos of their grandchildren, prayers from them and their families; they expected no replies from me. They were a light in my darkest days. Each time I received something and was well enough to check my phone, I would smile and feel lucky. They wanted me to know my life at home was still there and they were waiting for me. It felt incredible.

Christmas Day 2016 was a day to add to these special moments and I would always remember it alongside all the other moments of love and support.

New Year, New Bone Marrow

Three weeks flew by. It was now time to face what was always going to be the most formidable. At every step I had been warned that this was the real challenge and it would test me. Not this final week of treatment so much, but what was to come after. I imagined I would be a mess when coming face to face with it. Waiting had been as hard as doing, and it had been a part of my life for far too long. I was too susceptible to infections and in the past week, I had developed thrush all over my stomach and back, immune suppression always being the gateway for this and every other infection which wanted to set up house. I had hoped it would not delay treatment. I was relieved when I was told they would just keep a close eye on it. Sanjay dropped past to see if I felt ready. I told him this time that I was. I'd come this far, let's do it, I said, surprising myself.

I had a central line inserted into my neck in the same

anaesthetic bay of recovery where I had had my Vascath inserted. This was less invasive than a Vascath and was carried out with no real issue. Though never comfortable, it was part of the norm now to have some sort of venous access created.

Today was a day of eight-hour chemo. This would be a serious attack on my bone marrow along with any residual traces of disease. It was intended to wipe my bone marrow out; with it the history of immunity that it held would disappear. In time, I would have to have all childhood immunizations again as I would have newborn bone marrow that held no resistance. But today and the week ahead were about destruction. I was started on all the prophylactic drugs to combat the side effects.

After day one, I simply felt weary.

Day two, like the day before, was also eight hours and all things considered, it seemed to go smoothly. Nausea rose and fell with the relief of cyclizine being administered four-hourly. The next two days introduced new drugs, which were not hung for as long. I was starting to feel very tired, however, and somewhat frail, but was proud of the way I was holding up. The final day was the most challenging. I was to suck ice for three hours. I had tried to prepare myself by imagining how long three hours could feel whilst sucking ice. I was to find out that it's a hell of a long time. The rooms, already kept cold, seemed freezing when sucking ice hour upon hour, making sure the ice touched all parts of my mouth and gums. Up behind my top lip, around over the inside of my cheeks, all over my tongue, in front of my bottom teeth. Over and over again, hour after hour. I was shivering, and Elisabeth wrapped me in a blanket. I took a cup of ice with me while Elisabeth took me for a roam around the gardens in the wheelchair, hoping the sun on my skin would make it easier. It did help, but it was exhausting. Finally, it was done. Elisabeth gave me a huge hug and told me I had done amazingly well.

Back in my room I hopped into bed, covered myself with a heavy blanket Kate had bought me to counter the cold of the hospital rooms and lay there listening to Elisabeth telling me it was over. I'd done it. Five days I had feared for so long were over. No more chemo. And hopefully no mouth ulcers after the effort of the last three hours. I was given a dose of cyclizine and with Elisabeth rubbing my hands to warm them, I fell asleep.

*

The next day was a day's rest. In between sleep, I tried to walk with my drip stand, up and down the ward hallway with the help of Philippa. It was a surreal feeling whenever I was filled with chemo drugs. I felt like me, yet I didn't. I was on the outside looking in. I looked at all the faces passing me in the hall, expecting they were looking at my remembrance of my own face, a head of hair and healthy complexion. Returning to my room and going to the toilet, I always shocked myself when I looked at my sallow face, my eyes sunken into my head, absolutely no hair on my head, no eyelashes, no eyebrows. I, like most others on the ward, looked very ill. I was in my own room again due to my susceptibility to infection, so seeing others in the hallway reminded me of the universal suffering on the ward. It could tend to feel like a solitary journey, but of course, many others surrounded me. Each had their own story of despair, sadness, fear and hope. I was grateful of these reminders and always tried to remember others in the ward when praying. The discussions about the next day's transplant began that evening, one nurse smiling as she told me, 'It's your birthday tomorrow.' Responding to my confused face, she told me everything was new from tomorrow, starting over with new bone marrow. Somehow that felt exciting, even though I really didn't understand why.

*

Mid-morning of the next day, the bags of my harvested bone marrow were brought to my room in a frozen casing. Water was brought to the right temperature and the bags were dipped in one at a time, until they were soft enough to be hung and connected to my central line. There was no pump and the bone marrow entered my line purely by gravity. As it travelled around my body, I became very hot, feeling quite odd across the chest and a little faint. It wasn't comfortable, and I looked forward to the third and final bag finishing. Once it had, it wasn't long before I started feeling better, and I realised that I had finally completed what had seemed so insurmountable. This strange hour or so was what it had all been about. This was transplant. I could feel how medically miraculous it was to be able to change a person's bone marrow. It must have taken years of research, many disappointments and then finally success. But for a patient, it was all about its life-giving potential. And in the shadows of this potential was the statistic that only forty per cent succeed to five years. This long, difficult road would result in a maybe. I had fallen from a great height when re-diagnosed and the shock was still reverberating throughout my body. I now felt too scared to assume that transplant would save me. I had done it because I wanted to live. I had given myself the best chance, but I knew that from now on, life would seem temporary. Success depended both on my ability to ride out recovery and on the tenacity of my disease. For now I just had to hang on for what would come until my infant bone marrow matured and was able to protect me once again. I was, and would be for some time, a sponge for any surrounding bacteria and germs. It had been a tiring day and all these thoughts were the devil's playground while I was so tired. I made myself lie back and absorb the fact that there would be no more chemo and tonight I would go to sleep with no cancer in my body.

What Couldn't Be Understood

My girls went home, and like me, thought they would return in a short while to take me home. None of us had really understood what the medical team meant when they said that post-transplant was the 'tricky' time. It is not the same for everyone, but I believe most become quite ill.

My journey with this started with the promised diarrhoea, every two to three minutes at first. At my physical peak, this would have been wearing, but feeling breathless and nauseated made it a true challenge. Eventually it slowed to about every half hour but was still all-consuming. Then slowly, over the coming days, I found it hard to swallow. I was low in certain minerals but was unable to swallow any tablets. Whether it was physically accurate or not, it felt as if my throat was swollen. Everything had to be given through my central line. I couldn't drink and finally I was unable to eat. I lay in darkness for days, a bag of light brown milky liquid hanging on my drip stand which was changed with great caution every twenty-four hours to avoid infecting the line. This was to feed me. I also had bags of fluid hung to keep me hydrated.

I remember my central line dressing being changed and I remember people coming and going throughout each day. The tea lady with glasses of Sustagen, the dietitian asking me if I could eat or drink anything at all, Jeremy asking if I felt well enough to chat and nurses asking if I could try and sit up so I didn't get pneumonia. I was unable to comply with any of these requests even though I tried. I just drifted in and out of sleep, periodically woken by diarrhoea or nausea. I remember a nurse putting drops in my mouth and asking me to swish them around, as I had developed thrush in my mouth. The team would come each day, but I could recall little about it. Rick and Bron would also visit me daily, but again, I could say little. I just lay in the dark.

In the middle of one night whilst having my routine obs, I was told I had a fever – the enemy of the immune-suppressed. Lights turned on and a doctor was summoned to draw blood from a vein and not the line.

(Blood couldn't be taken from the line in case it was the line itself that was infected.) My veins had disappeared after months of chemo and it was a struggle to find one.

These bouts of fever would occur regularly; each time blood tests were done and reported on, antibiotics were hung and hourly observations to monitor temp and blood pressure initiated. At one of these routine observations, a code was called in my room and I heard my room number called over the speakers in the ward. Doctors and nurses rushed to my room as my blood pressure had apparently dropped dangerously low. All these incidences drove me to believe that I was losing. It was too much.

One morning as I opened my eyes, I saw Kate in the corner chair in my room, sitting in the dark with me. I learned later she had come as they had told her I was very ill. Time was difficult to gauge, but I sensed that I'd been in this state for many days. It broke my heart to see her there. One day I noticed she had left. I presumed she'd gone home and I felt so very sad for not being able to comfort her at all. At some point, I'm not sure how long into this hospital stay, I started feeling more alert, and nurses started to help me shower as I had not washed for days. Time was still indistinct though and I felt quite confused as to when it was day or night. My breathing was hugely labored, and I had a cough that was becoming worse. Diarrhoea continued sporadically at three or four times per day, still requiring an adult nappy.

I was being asked to eat but the sight or smell of any food was just overwhelming, and I felt like dry retching. They were unable to disconnect me from IV food until I could eat sufficiently. At first eating was only possible if I was to have cyclizine straight after. Having it before the food did nothing. But after, it dealt with the immense nausea that came from swallowing whatever I could manage. Most days it was two to three teaspoons of corn flakes. Bringing the spoon to my mouth was a monumental task, with my stomach writhing at the thought of what was coming.

This one morning, I had got out of bed and tried to comply with everyone's hopes for me to shower, change and sit in a chair to have breakfast. My lungs were struggling even more and felt as if they were infected. But I wanted to do what I could to get stronger and this was the first step. As I sat trying to eat, suddenly in came Dean. When he saw me, he just said, 'Oh, darling,' and hugged me. His eyes filled with tears. I cried to see him.

We were both weeping at what I had become.

*

With Dean's help each day, I worked hard at trying to eat. It really was one of the hardest things I had ever done. I just didn't want to, and my body let me know with force that it didn't want to be disturbed with food. It was a hellish job to finally eat enough that the team were willing to disconnect me from the liquid food feeding into my line. It would take me a good six months before my appetite would return in even the slightest way, but at least while I was eating enough to be disconnected, I was getting closer to going home to Rick's.

These days were difficult, consistently trying to maintain some sort of food intake with lungs that were sore and working hard for every breath. It was freezing in my room and I would sit wrapped in Kate's blanket by the window. Coughing brought on gagging that made me feel like I would pass out. It was a seemingly endless cycle, which unlike normal illnesses in the parallel world, did not improve a little each day but seemed to repeat monotonously, like Ground Hog Day. It was hard to imagine wellness ever again. My niece would bring me a thermos of reconstituted tinned tomato soup, which tasted like caviar in contrast to the hospital food. Bronwyn would bring me some homemade chicken soup, which probably gave me more nourishment than everything I had eaten in my whole hospital stay. However, strength still did not come and finally, after a five-week admission, I was told to go home and try and see how I managed.

Dean picked me up and whilst I was elated to be out of the hospital, I knew from the first steps that I wasn't well enough to be there, at Rick's place. Following one very breathless night, I was readmitted to Day Ward and put on a nebuliser. After another difficult night I was given a controlled sputum test to try and find the origin of my lung issues. I once again returned to Rick's. (Dean had left Western Australia by now.) I tried to manage using my nebuliser throughout the day and night as I waited for my results. When I next saw David he told me I had aspergillus. I walked again to the hospital pharmacy, from chair to chair, panting at each break. Again, I feared my heart would not manage and it beat hard. At one point I sat down on a couch and thought I might collapse. I saw Sanjay and called out to him and just started to sob. He sat and held my hand and told me he understood how I felt, but I *would* get better. It just would take some time. I looked at him helplessly, feeling so alone and desperate. I was so grateful to have him sitting with me for what seemed like half an hour. He gave me courage to find my way to the taxi phone and get myself home.

Losing God

Filled with the comfort of Sanjay's words, I went home and tried to change my mindset. But in the middle of the night, I felt like I had broken glass passing through my bowels. I bounced off the walls as I walked to the bathroom, sat and tried to relieve the pain by going to the toilet. After what seemed like interminable diarrhoea, nothing seemed to help. I slid onto the floor and just sobbed. The next day I returned to hospital. I was told that I had developed CMV. Not sure what this was, I was made aware that no nurse who was pregnant could look after me. Elisabeth was newly pregnant and couldn't come, and without her, Philippa couldn't come either. Dean was flat out at work and couldn't leave, as was Kate.

Some hours later I went into renal failure and was catheterised. The vicar came around and I begged her to say a prayer over me as I felt I had lost my connection to

God and sensed I was close to the end.

These days were my lowest. The team was amazing. Without them I'm sure I would have given up. My disconnection from God terrified me, as I feared dying alone, without His comfort. These days would scar me; even though there were still months of recovery ahead, these terrible moments determined the rest.

*

The next few months brought the slowest, most difficult recovery. But slowly it came. I walked to regain strength, on strong cytotoxic drugs to kill all the infections, which only heightened the nausea, trying to wean myself off the only anti-nausea drug, which worked so I could go home. It was a lot. I think it took from February to April. It broke me in the truest sense. My body slowly rallied, but this time, my heart would not heal. I tried. But it was just too much over the full nine years of cancer and I was emotionally spent. I returned home and tried to embrace the relief of others amidst the despair I felt.

In April, I returned to Sydney and soon after, to my work as a therapist. I had changed. I didn't have as much to give. I was constantly weeping inside if not overtly. PTSD, they labelled it. I don't much believe in labels. I just think in the end, cancer treatment broke my heart. Everyone has a capacity for only so much. Some, far braver than I, manage so much better. I felt, with some shame, this was it for me.

I had some special days, including the birth of my darling little Charlie in September, healthy and thank God unaffected by my CMV infection. In March I learned that Philippa would have another little one later in the year. These truly were blessings and, both intellectually and emotionally, they meant a great deal. But I felt like a shell; my heart was beating yet I wasn't *alive*. I was trying to engage in a world that took too much effort, only to be cast back into a place of re-diagnosis at any moment. The disappointment was so great that it was safer to stay ready for the shoe to drop.

I turned sixty in this time, a number I must say I didn't think I'd reach. It felt like a small victory. My family and friends gave me such a celebration and I took stock of all the meaning and love that surrounded me. I had much to be grateful for. I had engaged with cancer for far too long. It was the loudest thing in my life. I had let it be. I needed to quiet it. I needed to notice what else was going on.

A few days later, over a lunch with Dean, Helen and my mother to celebrate my birthday quietly, at a restaurant that Elisabeth married in, I was reminded I didn't control much. We sat and I enjoyed the beautiful beachfront view on a beautiful Sunday. Suddenly my dish was brought to me. A dish I didn't remember ordering. Helen toasted me happy birthday. I looked at Dean and asked if it was May. Was it my birthday month? Yes, he replied. For a moment I sat confused, then all seemed to return to normal and I just tried to let go of the odd feeling that I had lost a few moments.

One Tuesday in June

A few weeks later something extraordinary happened. I woke up, had my breakfast and tea, and sat down at my desk. I had begun posting on social media for my therapy business again and I had to write an article for the quarterly newsletter. I had been examining the need to notice what was going on aside from the clank of cancer in my brain. I wrote an article on coexistence of emotions – those whispers that reside beneath the noise. The kiss of a loved one, a hug of a child, the joy of a lovely meal. Moments spent with people that matter sharing things that matter. Illness is loud, but there are always whispers. I was determined to start noticing the whispers with greater mindfulness.

I posted the article to Facebook, sent it to our subscribers and pulled the door to my study shut.

*

My next recollection was of lying in a ward in hospital, being asked if I knew where I was, who I was, what I did for a living, what year it was. They told me they thought I had had a stroke. I had lost about forty-eight hours. I had apparently called Elizabeth that Tuesday evening saying I felt confused. Then she and Philippa took over. To this day, I haven't recollected those hours and it was a miracle I had the thought to phone someone, seeing I had no idea what was actually happening.

Whilst I had been feeling physically strong up to that Tuesday, when I started to become aware of my surroundings in hospital, I realised I was completely exhausted. I had immense nausea and was receiving IV drugs to quieten it. I had raised glands in my armpits and neck, was tested daily for heart, neurological and lymphoma symptoms. I had a hole in my heart. Who knew? All that I never thought possible had become so. Why not that, too? It seemed strangely irrelevant to me, even though it worried the doctors. I felt like there were too many things unravelling at once and I simply couldn't invest in what any one of them meant. Still, as a chorus they seemed to be telling me something.

I lay in a hospital bed for two and a half weeks and

finally was told there would be a meeting at 3pm on a particular day to have a chat. I had had a PET the day before and really didn't want to know the results before the meeting. I wanted another night without news of any sort.

That night I prayed for healing. They say you should pray specifically. Yes, I wanted healing. No more maybes, no more percentiles, no more hope that could be dashed. I didn't pray with expectation. I prayed with a naked heart. Now God held the answer and I would learn it.

Holding My Own Hand out of the Maze

There were no surprises in what came that day and yet we all sobbed with the grief, our fears confirmed as fact. A long report in my doctor's hand let me know that I was again in the hands of lymphoma. Dean, Elisabeth and I felt the pain of it deeply. In that moment, I knew something in my own heart that the others didn't. I knew this despite any further promises of treatment solutions. My body was broken. I had had renal failure, lung damage, a stroke, my gut was always nauseated, and whatever benefit further chemo or trials may have on the lymphoma, my body and spirit just couldn't take it. I asked how long with no treatment and was told a few months. I had a grandchild due in four. That cut through me like a knife.

In this moment everything I had learned about humanity coalesced into a single need for self-determination and care for my soul.

Thirtieth percentiles of success meant nothing to me any longer. I had given my body to medicine and it had done its best. But I now wanted to protect my failing organs from more of the same. I wanted to die as me and this meant preserving whatever health I could in the midst of the lymphoma. I wanted to make peace with it and see if surrendering to the disease made the remaining days more gentle.

This journey for me had always been about the medical profession finding the eyes of the human being and connecting. Seeing the need beneath and not just the disease. Shouldn't I now offer myself just the same? I had never felt surer of anything.

Over the next few weeks I had many conversations with my girls and they found a place to love me enough to let me rest in my truth. I will never know how to repay them that love.

I write these final pages whilst I'm quite weak, but each day I see faces of people I love, and it brings me joy. For that I am so deeply grateful.

I hope this book gives a perspective of one woman's journey. I know it's so different for all and would never prescribe a path, other than to say choose a team that understands the human journey into this frightening world of cancer. For me, it changed everything.

Finally, to my most beloved girls: let go of cancer now. It has lived with you far too long. A mother could not have been loved or supported through these years better than I have been. It's enough now. I want it out of your lives and for you to have boundless joy with your children and husbands. This is my deepest wish for you.

You have been the light of my days from the moment you were all born. I loved you then, I love you now and I will love you always.

Post Script

As I read the close of my book, I realise the abruptness with which it ends. This is in fact how it felt in living it. An abrupt end to a long and winding journey into the unknown. Since moving into palliation, I have had much to say to my loved ones that I feared another stroke might prevent. Now I have done this; the story is written. And now I would like to say my thanks to those who fulfilled my deepest plea at the outset of becoming ill: a plea for respect, compassion and integrity. I wish to thank the human beings who saw my spirit and held it respectfully. To them, I owe everything.

David Joske and all his team, Dominic from Pall care, Mark Hertzberg and Richard Chye and his team, and Lucy, 10 West's most amazing NUM.

I leave each of you as a grateful recipient of your humanity. I encourage you, at every registrar rotation, to let your colleagues know that they have the ability to sustain the spirit of those patients whose bodies are broken by cancer. Not via platitudes and condescension, but through honest, respectful listening to what each autonomous being needs in order to feel of value, to feel safe and to determine their own very unique path alongside their care team. You hold the power of great change.

Unending gratitude, Karina

Final Note

As expressed by mum in her own words, being told that she most likely would not meet her fourth grandchild who was due in September, 2018, was extremely painful for her and for us all.

On 25th September, 2018, baby Riley was born. Mum held on with such determination through her last days and on 26th September, 2018, mum finally met her new grandson. The following day on 27th September, 2018, our beautiful mum passed away.